FRONTIERS OF NEW TOURISM

FRONTIERS OF NEW TOURISM

M. P. BEZBARUAH

GYAN PUBLISHING HOUSE
NEW DELHI-110 002

FRONTIERS OF NEW TOURISM
(Tourism)

Rs. 360

ISBN : 81-212-0747-9

Published in 2002 in India by
Gyan Publishing House
5, Ansari Road, New Delhi-110002

Phones : 3261060, 3282060, Fax : 3285914
E-Mail : gyanbook@del2.vsnl.net.in
Website: http:\\www.gyanbooks.com

Cover photo (mighty Brahmputra & clouds) and
Back cover (tea garden of North - East India)
designed by Phal S. Girota, PQRS (India)

Lasertypesetting by : Varsha Graphics, Delhi
Printed at : Chawla Offset Printers, Delhi

Dedicated to

the memory of

a remarkable lady

'Ma'

(late Manorama Bhattacharyya)

Contents

FOREWORD

After having the privilege of writing the foreword for Mr. M.P. Bezbaruah's book titled "Indian Tourism – Beyond the Millennium", I feel doubly honoured to be called upon to write another one for "Frontiers of New Tourism". Mr. Bezbaruah could not have chosen a more appropriate topic to write about, because he has aptly linked the subject-matter of the first book with that of the present one. Undoubtedly, a millennium can only be pregnant with opportunities as well as challenges in all spheres of life including tourism.

As was noted in "Indian Tourism – Beyond the Millennium", India's tourism potential is as great as the country is vast. However, the wide range of tourism products that India has to offer remains largely unexplored. These range from thousands of ancient monuments and archaeological remains to its diverse topography, races, customs and traditions, languages, festivals, dances and gastronomy. The Himalayan States such as Himachal Pradesh, Jammu & Kashmir offer opportunities for mountaineering and heli-skiing; sailing and cruising can be practised in Kerala's backwaters; Goa, Lakshdweep, the Andaman and Nicobar Islands offer water-sports and beach holidays. Other tourist attractions that can be cited are the cold desert and the Buddhist monasteries of Ladakh, as well as India's many bird sanctuaries and wildlife.

The World Tourism Organisation's forecast of 1.6 billion international tourist arrivals by the year 2020 places Asia as the second region to be the most visited in the world inspite of the financial crises it underwent a few years ago. This projected growth of tourist arrivals world-wide will have a two-sided effect: it will undoubtedly enhance the bright side of tourism which has endeared it to countries, but at the same time, it will pose the challenge of managing the avalanche of visitors who will flock to tourist attractions.

India's cultural heritage, which is embodied in its numerous age-old monuments, and the customs and the traditions of its people are equally going to experience their share of the pressure that the increase in international tourist arrivals is going to produce.

If India is to have its fair share of the tourism prospects projected for the next twenty years, two major issues will have to be addressed: first, the main constraints that militate against the exploitation of India's full tourism potential, have to be minimised considerably; second, strategies have to be devised to ensure a balance between tourism development and the physical and cultural environment on which it depends for its very existence. State Governments, in partnership with trade bodies need to devise effective measures in this direction.

Mr. Bezbaruah is an outstanding figure in the Indian Ministry of Tourism and his contribution to its tourism development has gained him renown not only within India but also in international circles. For instance, he was the Chairman of Pacific Asia Travel Association (PATA). Furthermore, his contribution to WTO's activities has always been noteworthy, especially since India became re-elected as a Member of the Executive Council at the 12th Session of the General Assembly, which was held in Istanbul, Turkey in 1997. In view of the close ties between Mr. Bezbaruah and WTO in general, and with me on a personal level, I am only too willing to recommend this volume, which is a testimony to his untiring efforts to enrich the tourism literature of our times. "Frontiers of New Tourism" offers its readers an insight into the steps to take to counteract unpalatable side of the flood of tourists to India's invaluable patrimony. The guidelines given transcend the context of India because of its applicability to cultural artefacts and heritage sites around the globe.

OMT. WTO. BTO

Francesco Frangialli
Secretary – General
World Tourism Organisation

PREFACE

My first book on tourism "Indian Tourism – Beyond the Millennium" was the result of my desire to know more about this important and fascinating sector. My present book, in essence, is a continuation of the same journey of exploration. This journey has not always been a happy one, but has invariably been a rewarding experience. I had moments of joy and happiness, interspersed with periods of a sense of frustration and despair. But, all in all, a good learning experience.

In this book, I am trying to go beyond the Indian context to look at the global scenario, as it is today and as it is likely to emerge in the future. It is not an exhaustive and academic study; nor is it intended to be. I have tried to savour the nuances of the biggest industry of the 21st Century and have briefly touched on the major issues, as I see them, that are likely to shape the character and the content of global tourism. Naturally, I have also tried to assess the relevance of these global developments to the Indian situation.

I am deeply indebted to Mr. Francesco Frangialli, Secretary General of the World Tourism Organization (WTO) who, as in the case of my first book, greatly inspired me by readily agreeing to write a comprehensive foreword to this book as well. I have benefited greatly from my personal meetings with him in the Executive Council of the WTO as well as in the meetings of the Strategic Group of the WTO. I am also grateful to Shri Ananth Kumar, former Minister of Trouism, Government of India, for kindly allowing me to use some of the published and unpublished documents of the Ministry. Mr. Jean-Claude

Baumgarten, President of the World Travel and Tourism Council (WTTC), has been a great source of inspiration for India in general and for me, in particular, and I must thank him sincerely for so readily allowing me to use all the WTTC publications, a privilege that I have used extensively.

The support and assistance of Shri Inder Jeet Mittal at every stage of the evolution of this book has been invaluable. He went about the laborious work of proof reading with meticulous care, making it possible for the book to come to its present form.

Shri D.D. Dhingra, Shri J.P. Malhotra and all members of my personal staff, rendered valuable direct or indirect support; Shri Madan Lal, in particular, did a very competent job of the entire dictation of the book.

In a sense, this book marks the second step in the fulfilment of my promise to my dear daughters – Supriya and Supirti – to try to make amends for my unfulfilled academic ambitions. However, due perhaps to their very high regard for my capabilities, they feel that I am still far from fulfilling my promise. The support of my wife Anuradha has been all encompassing. Her perceptive comments about the style and the language have changed the quality and the complexion of the book.

I was touched by the reception to my first book. If this one also can contribute, however little it may be, to creating awareness about tourism, I will feel that my efforts have been worthwhile. This will give me the feeling of having returned in a small measure, my gratitude to a sadly neglected sector which has given me so much of a sense of belonging, involvement, and satisfaction during my final years of public service.

M.P. Bezbaruah

ACKNOWLEDGEMENTS

Ministry of Tourism, Government of India

- for allowing the use of all published and unpublished documents.

World Tourism Organization (WTO)

World Travel and Tourism Council (WTTC)

- for allowing the use of their published documents.

1

TOURISM - FUTURE CHALLENGES AND OPPORTUNITIES

"Time present and time past
Are both perhaps present in time future
And time future contained in time past"

T.S. Eliot
(Burnt Norton, Four Quartets)

History, it is often said, repeats itself. Many philosophers think that the future is just the projection of the past. Spengler saw a pattern in the rise and fall of civilizations. According to Arnold Toynbee, history followed a pattern and, therefore, a scientific study and a logical projection about the future, is possible.

Yet, the beauty and excitement about the future lie in its unpredictability.

The history of the world is replete with the stories of famous predictions going wrong. Some delightful anecdotes often quoted are –

* Thomos Watson, Chairman of the IBM said in 1943- "I think there is a world market for may be 5 Computers."

* Even in 1977, Ken Olson, President, who was the Chairman and the founder of Digital Equipment Corporation, said –
  "There is no reason anyone would want a computer in their home."

* A Yale University Professor who had seen Fred Smith's paper on alternative strategy for overnight services in the postal delivery system wrote-
  "The concept is interesting but the idea must be feasible if it is to get a grade better than 'C'."
  Frad Smith went on to establish the Federal Express Corporation, the hugely successful multi-national organization in alternative postal delivery services.

* The famous Decca Recording Company in 1962 rejected the Beatles thinking that "guitar music was on the way out" and the Beatles went on to make history.

An assessment of the future of tourism, however, should start with a look at the present scenario and the process of its evolution.

The growth of international tourism was slow in the first part of the last Century, rapid in the later part and phenomenal since 1980s. In 1950, the total arrival was only 25 million generating receipts of $2.1 billion. The absolute number of arrivals multiplied two and a half times between 1960 and 1970 and thereafter it has almost doubled every decade. The receipts from tourism have grown even faster, $18 billion in 1970 increased to $105 billion in 1980. It is well known now that as a contributor to the global economy, tourism has no equal. In 2000, the arrivals reached 698 million with total international tourism receipt of $476 billion. Over the past 15 years, international tourism receipts have grown 1.5% faster than world GDP[1]. John Naisbitt, in his book "Global Paradox", had estimated in 1994 that with about $ 3.4 trillion of output, it was the largest industry in the world.[2] According to the World Tourism Organization (WTO), "In 1998 international tourism accounted for an estimated 8 percent of the world's total export earnings and 37 percent of exports in the services sector. International tourism receipts and passenger transport amounted to more than $ 504 billion, putting it ahead of all other categories of international trade as shown below[3] :

S.No.	Category of Trade	$ billion
1.	International Tourism	504
2.	Automotive products	496
3.	Chemicals	490
4.	Food	458
5.	Petroleum and other fuels	435
6.	Computers and office equipment	394
7.	Textiles and clothing	332
8.	Telecommunications equipment	279
9.	Mining products	163
10.	Iron and steel	141

Many issues and factors have contributed to this growth outlined above, some directly others indirectly. The tremendous changes in the civil aviation sector starting from the 60s along with introduction of wide bodied jet propulsion aircraft making travel easier and faster, was the beginning of the story. Rapid developments in the world economy and particularly the emergence of the Asian Tigers, propelled this growth in the 80s. Many of the developing countries also saw better performance in economic development in the 80s and 90s, making available huge amounts of income for leisure and travel.

During this period, incredible changes have taken place in the geo-political situations in the world which have helped to make this growth possible. As Naisbitt has pointed out foremost among some change were the developments in the Soviet Union and Eastern Europe which have released huge resources blocked up in arms race and cold war. Suddenly, therefore, the changes in international diplomatic and political configurations have added 430 million East - European and former Soviet Union citizens – larger than the population of Western Europe – to the category of potential travellers. The decades of the 70s and the 80s have improved the perception of the travellers about safety in travels. End of the Korean and Vietnam wars has paved the way for the Asia - Pacific region to emerge as the highest growth area in world tourism.

All these developments have contributed to making travels easier and, therefore, have changed our perceptions about travel.

Added on to this changed environment was the beginning of a process of economic liberalization in countries like China and India which account for 38 percent of the total world population. For example, the liberalisation process has helped growth of outbound tourists from India and today about 4 million Indians are travelling abroad. China is emerging as a very important source of outbound markets in the world, and by the WTO estimates, would generate 100 million outbound tourists by 2020[4].

The emergence of European Union and the dismantling of borders in Europe, as every one knows, has also been a major development. Naisbitt has mentioned that "tourism is the force that will make global village truly one world." Constitution of free zones, dismantling of visa formalities, growth of regional alliances are some of the developments which are likely to influence tourism growth patterns in the future. Countries and regions failing to respond to such challenges will be at a disadvantage and are likely to be left behind in the new competitive scenario. Europe, with the single currency 'Euro' gets many advantages because the single currency is-

Simple - tourist need to carry only one currency;

Transparent - it allows easy comparison across borders; and

Economical - allow economy in changing and rechanging dollars and pounds and also in the time that is spent in doing so[5].

Similarly, creation of several free trade areas, largest being the NAFTA (North American Free Trade Association) – world's largest free trade area between Canada, Mexico and USA - also has influenced the travel and tourism scenario.

A WTO Study in 1990[6] had analysed the influences that would affect the growth of tourism during the 90s. It had projected a figure of 638 million arrivals and $ 527 billion in receipts by 2000. The broad forecasts about the trends have materialised. The arrivals have exceeded the projections though there has been a shortfall in earnings.

It is significant that at present the total international arrival of tourists represents only about 7 percent of the potential and capable travellers of the world's total population. Therefore, the potential for future growth is immense. Even 1 percent increase in the number of potential travellers actually travelling would add 100 million to the total arrivals.

John Naisbitt in his book "Global Paradox" has analysed some of the influences which are likely to shape the future of the world. He has couched his observation in paradoxes - all full of more meanings than what is apparent, reminiscent of Alices Adventures in Wonderland. Some of these observations have implications for the future of tourism, which as is commonly mentioned, has made the world a global village, viz., -

> "As the global economy gets larger its component parts get smaller".
>
> "Think locally, act globally" is the new slogan.
>
> "As the importance of the nation State recedes, more of them are being created"[7].

Naisbitt's observations and generalisations drawn from observed trends, need to be carefully analysed as these developments will give shape to the growth of tourism in the future. It is most likely that globalization of tourism - the biggest industry of the future, will be increasingly driven by the smallest player, the individuals, whose choices and preferences will guide and control the industry.

At the same time, the more competitive the world becomes in tourism, the more each country will try to focus on the authenticity of its distinctiveness. "The bonding commonality of human beings is our distinctiveness" (Naisbitt)[8]. Every country will try to pronounce its distinctiveness to attract more and more tourists.

The significance of these observations for policy formulation and development of strategy, will be apparent when we examine the compulsive influences that will guide the future of tourism.

However, we need to qualify our observations about the future because tourism forecasts suffer from some inherent difficulties. 'The Economist' in 1993 in its 'Survey of World Travel and Tourism' scenario had summed up these difficulties very aptly –

Firstly, there is no accepted definition of "Tourism" as such – or what constitutes "Tourism". It comprises of so many activities which differ in import and content from country to country that a common denominator is difficult to find. The World Travel and Tourism Council (WTTC) has identified upwards of 30 activities to be at the core of tourism business. The following illustration used by WTTC explains the difficulties:-

TIP OF AN ECONOMIC ICEBERG

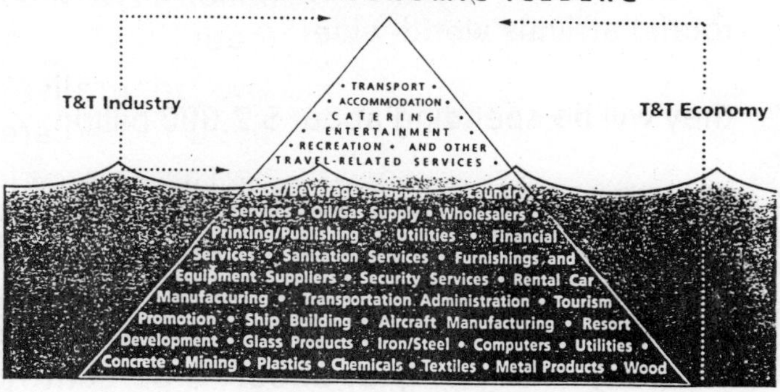

Secondly, many of the activities can't be easily quantified and are not measurable and, therefore, tend to be left out; and

Thirdly, International comparison is "bedevilled" says the Economist, "by astounding differences" in the method of data collection and interpretation. In recent years, efforts by the WTO and the UN to develop a standardized, comparable set of statistics through Tourism Satellite Account System has resulted in some improvements in the system of accounting. Countries which have accepted this method have realised the great economic impact of tourism, which otherwise remains concealed. But, the problems of establishing the economic importance of tourism, in general, persist.

In spite of these difficulties, based on sample surveys, the World Tourism Organization and the World Travel and Tourism Council have been able to make fairly accurate estimates. These estimates project astounding growth of travel and tourism during the coming decades. It is estimated that –

* by 2020 there will be 1.6 billion international tourist arrivals world-wide;

* they will be spending about $ 2,000 billion;

* the sustained annual average growth rate in Tourism will be 4.3 percent in arrivals and 6.7 percent in receipts – which is far above the probable expansion of the world's wealth, which will be growing only at about 3 percent per annum;

* between 1995 and 2005, 144 million new jobs would have been created in this sector – 112 million of them being in the Asia - Pacific region alone.[9]

And, all these will be achieved, as mentioned above, with only about 7 percent of the real potential travellers of the world population actually travelling. Tourism, it is rightly said, therefore, is "an industry truly still in its infancy"[10] holding immense potential for future growth.

How these potentials are actually realised will depend on the response of the industry to a number of major influences. Mr. Francesco Frangialli, the then Deputy Secretary General and (present Secretary General) of W.T.O., in his incisive Somnath Chib Memorial Lecture in New Delhi in 1994, summed up the major challenges which shaped tourism growth in the 90s and which were expected to exercise a much stronger influence in the coming years, in five groups, viz., –

(a) Socio–demographic factors
(b) Changes in consumer behaviour
(c) Technological changes
(d) Development strategies
(e) Human resource development

The salient features of these influences are briefly analysed below.

Socio-demographic changes

Socio-demographic changes in the later part of the Twentieth Century have been, in contrast to the earlier periods, very rapid and striking. Impact of some of these developments – both in the tourist generating and developed countries as well as in the developing countries – has been far-reaching from the point of view of tourism.

One of the major trends has been ageing of population and declining growth of population in the developed countries combined with increasing population and larger number of workforce in the developing countries. Because of declining population growth in the industralised countries, the share of the developed countries in the total world population is growing at a higher proportion. The pattern and pace of Gross Demostic Product (GDP) growth of these developing countries will have significant influences on the growth of outbound tourism markets in the future. Inspite of the general feeling that most of the developing countries may not be able to generate sufficient GDP for a substantial number of their population to engage in travel abroad, the impact of economic growth on the growing outbound tourism from China, India and many other South-East Asian countries is already discernible.

More important implications arise from the declining population of the developed countries which has resulted in the continued decline of the number of people between the age group of 15-20. The post-war birth bulge commonly referred to as the 'baby boom generation' born between 1946 and 1954 have reached the age groups with the highest propensity and financial ability to travel. This factor, combined with declining birth rates in the industralised countries in the 1960s and 1970s and a greater life expectancy, has resulted in the middle-aged and the elderly constituting a higher proportion of tourist population. It was estimated by the WTO that, by 2000, U.K. should have more than 20 million people over the age of 50, who will account for 30% of all holiday spending by the British.[11] The WTO Report also estimated that as a direct consequence, the volume of beach holidays taken by the British will fall by 1 million by 2005. Naisbitt has summed up this trend beautifully : "Blessed with good health, good pension plans, and new found freedom, the over 55s of the world are taking to the highways, to the air and to the sea."[12] He has estimated that by 2010, the population above 55 in USA will increase to 27% of the total. The Time Magazine Survey of June 16, 1997 reported: "Wheatcroft projects that travel to Europe by older Americans will rise by nearly 80% this decade and predicts Europeans will follow suit." Says the Economist: 'all the evidence shows that older people are now more adventurous. People aged 70 and 80 don't regard themselves as being old'."[13] Socio-demographic studies also reveal that most of these prospective tourists are better educated, have greater flexibility in using their leisure time and have increasing volume of leisure time. Therefore, they are looking for greater and better travel experiences unlike in the past. There is no doubt that the choices and preferences of this large group of tourists will change the complexions of tourism products in the future.

These socio-demographic factors are also leading to some other major developments. The importance and share of women in the workforce of the tourist-generating countries has been on the increase. This has resulted in two other significant developments in the nature and composition of the average households. There are more and more two income households and also an increasing number of single member families. They have more disposable income and also desire to travel but have less leisure time. This situation is generally alluded to as the "time-poor money rich" syndrome. It has several implications. One easily noticeable implication is that, instead of longer vacations, such families will be inclined to take several short vacations. It follows therefrom that a greater number of tourists would probably repeat such trips. Such repeat travellers are likely to be more discerning and sophisticated in their choice of the destinations as well as of the services they expect. More and more such travellers, particularly those who are self-employed, are tending to work not from any fixed office and tend to take thier office with them. Such travellers, in a sense, tend to combine work with pleasure and in such short repeated trips, will prefer places which have facilities that enable them to keep in touch with their work.

The economic and financial developments in the world also have, as only to be expected, great impact on the trends of travel. A WTO Study has commented on an interesting statistical relationship between growth of an economy and travel – "There is a clear link between travel trends and general economic developments. Travel growth is generally very sensitive to whether an economy is expanding, or is in a recessionary phase. Typically, if other factors such as relative prices are unchanged, a 1% growth rate in total real private consumption tends to be associated with a standstill in travel, 2.5% with a 4% expansion in travel, and a 5% growth in consumption with a 10% rate of increase in travel spending; at anything below 1% growth in consumption, travel usually falls, but responses for individual origin countries vary considerably from these averages".[14]

The 1980s had seen in an average about 3% growth rate of GDP of most industralised countries. The average annual growth rate during the 90s has been about the same. All future projections indicate that Personal Discretionary Disposable Income (PDDI) is likely to grow faster in the coming decade. Significantly and happily a larger proportion of the income growth is expected to be more widely distributed among the income groups. As a result, a larger proportion of the population will gain means to engage in travel and tourism, and a larger number of high income consumers are likely to be engaged in greater tourism activity and expenditure. To quote from the 'Time' Magazine Survey again - "People everywhere are increasingly discerning," says Brian Manning, General Manager of Asiaworld (U.K.), Asia's largest travel agency. "They want to travel independently. They want to put a tour together themselves and make their own choices. They want to travel on scheduled airlines. And they're prepared to pay for it." Asiaworld's success is shown by the fact that the cost of the average vacation sold by its British subsidiary is $2,900 a person. Says Manning: "In much of Europe, North America and Asia, there is more disposable income now than ever before in history."[15]

The WTO had estimated that by 2015, the workforce in the Third-World countries will expand by 700 million by which time the number of young workers in the industralised countries would either stagnate or decline. As a result, much of this workforce may be engaged in industrialised countries as human capital to sustain their economic growth. Increase in ethnic travels of such groups is expected to be a major factor in the growth of tourism in the coming years.

Implications of these factors for both outbound and inbound tourism would be significant. The markets will diversify faster and competition based on technological strength and quality of services would be much more intense than ever before. These trends which are becoming increasingly evident imply that tourism marketing policies would need to be constantly modified and should be so designed that they could respond and adjust to emerging trends quickly and without friction.

The National Tourism Organizations (NTOs) Survey of 85 countries by the WTO on the **Tourism 2020 Vision** showed a consistency in strategic thinking among countries, for the coming decades. The key priorities identified by NTOs are:

* Increased, more focused and more aggressive marketing.

* Constant striving for a competitive edge through a combination (usually of all three) of product differentiation, quality and/or price.

* Growing recognition of the need for sustainable tourism development to ensure long-term prosperity.

* Less State control, and more State/Private Sector partnerships.

The proposed plan of strategic action, at that point of time also reflected awareness of these newly emerging compulsions –

* "78 percent intend to focus their marketing strategy on key tourist generating markets, reducing the spread of their activities;

* 77 percent plan to utilise the approach of targeting their marketing at the most appropriate market segments;

* 88 percent will increase their overseas marketing activity;

* 90 percent intend to pursue cooperative marketing campaigns with the private sector;

* 77 percent believe their marketing approach will need to take a more aggressive, competitive stance."[16]

One major impact of these changes would be an increase in market segmentation. Thus, an increasing and intensifying competition at all levels to woo an ever-increasing number of more demanding and more knowledgeable tourists will undoubtedly lead to more and more market segmentation. It will be necessary, therefore, to devise micro marketing strategies and to develop quality of services that can sustain interest of the repeat visitors. Innovative enterprise and imaginative planning will shape the future marketing horizon. Some of the key growth market segments for future are expected to be –

(a) development of new destinations;
(b) market holidays that are tailored both in content and facilities to the specific tastes and demands;

(c) adventure travel combining two or more of the elements of environment, outdoor, nature, etc.;

(d) new experiences of mystic and spiritual content; and

(e) just short breaks designed purely for relaxation away from work place.

Technological developments

By far, the most profound challenges of the future will be of technological developments. If socio-demographic influences put the consumer – the tourist – in a more commanding position regarding his choices and preferences, the future technological developments are definitely going to strengthen this empowerment to make the consumer the 'king'. One distinctive feature of technological change is that it is developing. To quote Naisbitt again, "at an ever-accelerating rate of speed, with each new technology compounding the speed and capabilities of those that came before".[17] The sweep of technological development has been wide and ever-changing, erasing the dominance of time and space and making the world a little place. So far as travel and tourism are concerned, developments in two particular areas of technology are likely to have the biggest impact. One is the revolution in telecommunication and information technology and the other is the technological change in the civil aviation sector.

The tremendous impact of the possible developments in information technology has been dramatically expressed in a joke attributed to Randall L. Tobias, former Vice Chairman of AT&T, and quoted by Naisbitt –

"A theologian asked the most powerful supercomputer, 'Is there a God?' The computer said, it lacked the processing power to know. It asked to be connected to all the other computers in the world. Still, it was not enough power. So, the computer was hooked up to all the mainframes in the world, and then all the minicomputers, and to all the personal computers. And, eventually it was connected to all the computers in cars, microwaves, VCRs, digital watches and so on. The theologian asked for the final time, 'Is there a God?' And the computer replied: 'There is now!"[18]

In the near future, Naisbitt has pointed out, all the communication capabilities needed by man could be fitted on to the desk, in the car or in the palm of the hand.

Few years back, Bill Gates had reportedly remarked that education, health and tourism were the three most important areas for attention in the world in the future. While the reference to tourism, no doubt, was influenced by the growing impact of tourism as the largest industry of the world, possibly it also was an expression of the assessment that the travel and tourism would be one of the key sectors to be revolutionized by information technology developments.

These changes in information technology will have two immediate consequences.

Firstly, it will empower the consumer in such a way that in the future scenario, the consumer will really be the king.

Secondly, it will change the organisational pattern of the tourism business.

How the electronic technology will empower the consumer is illustrated by a few examples by the World Tourism Organization's Vision 2020 as follows:-

- "Smart card destination loyalty schemes where the user gets discounts for using the card at a destination and, in return, the destination gains valuable marketing information about its customers.

- Plastification of travellers' cheques, again using smart card technology.

- Internet video telephony whereby consumers can "test drive" a prospective holiday by viewing current pictures through cameras placed in hotels, clubs, restaurants, and other sites in the destination and transmitted via the Internet.

- Intelligent agent computer programmes which are a combination of pre-entered information (e.g. likes and dislikes in respect of holidays) and observed behaviours in use of on-line booking patterns to make suggestions on possible options for the user, thus saving time in "surfing" the Internet.

- CD ROMs are likely to be increasingly used as electronic brochures, saving time in the inspection of paper brochures. These are likely to be sponsored by both tour operators and destinations

- On-line booking via the Internet is certain to grow at rapid rates over the next decade with access available to most of the population of industrialised countries. Though transfer of such access to usership in respect of travel booking may take time, it is clear that this medium will achieve increasing uptake in the next 10 to 15 years.

- E-ticketing (or ticketless travel) is being operated, on a limited basis already, by a number of airlines (e.g. BA, SAS, United).

- Central databases of traveller information will provide extensive insight into individual traveller's preferences and behavioural patterns, and will be available on a commercial basis. One initial such scheme is being developed by Arthur Andersen and Pegasus Systems in respect of hotel customers."[19]

The increasing use of computer technology naturally wiil change relationship between the supplier, the intermediary and the consumer. Not only will the use of technology allow greater access to information to the travelling public, its application for global reservation system, interactive travel information, virtual reality experiences, will make the consumer more powerful in making his choices and in demanding his preferences.

Lord Marshall, Chairman of the British Airways, in his Somnath Chib Memorial Lecture in New Delhi in 1999 had pointed out that within the next five or six years, the industry is expected to progress to a stage where more than half of all international scheduled-journeys will be undertaken with new electronic tickets. How will it affect the Travel industry? Will the old-fashioned Travel agents wither away? There are not enough statistics to make a generalisation. But, it seems safe to say, on the basis of the changes that have been observed, that while the industry will change, in this service industry the human touch can't be completely dispensed with.

The use of global distribution system and computer reservation systems which are already dominating the travel and tourism scenario, is likely to be accelerated in the coming years. The process of globalisation, it is felt, will be accompanied by or directly lead to vertical integration of the travel business in the private sector. While this globalisation process provides many facilities and opportunities to the consumers and to the operators, it is not an unmixed blessing. The possible 'opportunities' and 'threats' of the system have been beautifully summed up by WTO as follows:-

"Opportunities	Threats
A. Travel Suppliers	
- product distribution in global markets at price to levels;	- CRS effectively reduces scope of airlines personalise their product and weaken their own product marketing initiatives.
- strategic links with other in suppliers can be re-enforced through the CRS (i.e. Through code sharing, connecting flights, etc);	- Control of the product is the hands of the CRS vendor not the airlines.
- yield management programmes enable airlines to carefully monitor and match supply:demand;	- Large airlines/groups of airlines are likely to threaten small/ medium sized airlines.
- airlines are in a position to price their seats precisely to what the market will bear in practice this means an increase in the number/ type of fares targeted at market segments.	

B. Travel Agents

- improved travel booking capabilities;	- Expensive to purchase and operate systems
- improved travel management reporting;	- Training requirement
- enhanced range of travel products to sell;	
- faster systems and "one stop" shopping approach;	- Agents need to select best system for their needs.
- interactive keyboard system permits non-travel booking functions such as word processing, etc.	

C. Consumers

- more efficient travel booking services;	- CRS system mergers could lead to control over pricing being held by a small number of travel service suppliers, resulting in a lack of competition and higher price levels.
- more travel information available;	
- greater opportunities to identify lower cost travel arrangements."[20]	

There is no doubt that the intensity and the extent of the use of such technological innovations will change the organizational structure of tourism industry and, therefore, of the tourism services. Already, the signs visible indicate that in the future, the travel and tourism sector will experience three types of major changes, namely, –

(a) horizontal integration of large operators forcing out the small and medium ones through economies of scale;

(b) vertical integration through acquisitions or alliances; and

(c) emergence of global multinationals in tourism business. Consequently, the playing arena for the industry is likely to be dominated by a small number of big operators and a large number of small operators – "niche players" taking care of the growing specialised markets.

If the period of the 60s and the 70s were revolutionized by the introduction of wide-bodied jet airlines, it will be changes in civil aviation technology again that will significantly change the travel and tourism business in the future. Lord Marshall, Chairman of the British Airways, in his Somnath Chib Memorial Lecture has drawn attention to some very key areas of such development. Not long into the next decade the estimated volume of present air passenger traffic of 1.4 billion of 1998 will have virtually doubled. This will pose great challenges for doubling the airport terminal facilities, surface access systems, hotel accommodation and so on. The support systems will have to be not only doubled but proportionately larger than it has been in the past. The concern for environmental and ecological issues being much more stringent than before, the new airports when they come up will have to be farther away from the metros. Therefore, all the support services will have to cover greater distances and will have to invest more in sustainable practices.

Mr. Marshall had also talked about Future Air Navigation Systems (FANS) which will iron out all the world's airways, so that one can fly in straight lines, reducing journey time and increasing efficiency. The annual cost savings and efficiency from such technological change are expected to be of the order of $10 billion. Similarly, the Future Automated Screening for Travellers (FAST) System which expedite immigration clearances using a Smart Card, based on biometrics devices, is already in operation. "We are much more likely to see the airframe manufacturing moving to the concept of mass hypersonic transport outside the earth's atmosphere turning the trip between Delhi and London to a short haul experience".[21] Marshall predicted that the future in aviation will be one of world alliance and partnership will be the way forward. Traditional systems of managing national civil aviation issues on notions of national sovereignty are likely to be less relevant in such a scenario, and also less tenable.

Many of these innovations are no longer in the realm of fancy and they are taking shape as distinct possibilities. For many countries such developments also pose future challenges of –

- ideology;
- getting together required resources;
- getting the suitable technology;
- putting in place the required safety norms; and
- the capacity to gear up to meet the sheer pressure of numbers.

Such technological developments will pose the greatest challenges to the ingenuity and innovativeness of marketing of destinations as well. Seamless global tourism information network, interactive videos creating virtual travel experiences for potential travellers and all other improvements following from technological developments will provide consumers with such opportunities that traditional marketing strategies will have to undergo complete change. Most countries, as noted already, have shown awareness of this inescapable reality.

Sustainable Development

While technological challenges and marketing needs in a changing scenario will require determined and calculated response, the future challenges in the spheres of safety and sustainability will need far wider coordination and attention. Such huge movements of tourists will raise issues of carrying and absorbing capacity of each destination. It will raise the issue of constant conflict between preservation and tourism promotio,n of present needs and future hopes, of pressures on the fragile eco-system, and non-renewable resources. Growth of tourism puts pressures on socio-cultural ethics and physical maintenance of heritage. The world has become a global village and in the process has also globalised problems of drugs and diseases. Such problems and challenges are not necessarily posed by tourism alone. Modern society faces many such challenges which come almost as corollary of progress. But, now there has been greater awareness, concern and resultant social activism against such adverse influences. Therefore, each country will be under closer scrutiny of the media and public organisations on such issues and each destination choice will be affected by the perception of the consumers about its performance on these parameters of human concern. Long-term success of tourism will largely depend on its sensitivity to sustainable development issues and in a narrower sense to the protection of and the use of the physical environment. But, it has been increasingly realised that what is only a concern now for sustainable development, will soon become an unavoidable requirement.

Such exponential growth of tourism as we have witnessed so far and as is predicted for the future, naturally will have its impact on the environment, ecology, culture, tradition and society. Broadly, unimaginative development of tourism can have a negative impact in three ways –

(a) On the eco-system – forest, wetlands, marine areas;
(b) impact on flora and fauna; and
(c) impact on local socio-cultural environment.

Environmental concerns are becoming increasingly louder all over the world. Reportedly, more than 5 million Americans travel overseas every year on nature-related trips and about 30 million Americans belong to various environmental organisations. Various world bodies are now alive to the concerns of sustainable development. Apart from the 'Agenda 21' adopted during the United Nations Conference on Environment and Development held in Rio de Janeiro, Brazil in June 1992, the United Nations Commission on Sustainable Development, the United Nations Environment Programme, the World Conservation Union, are all involved in various aspects of development of sustainable tourism. Such concerns find reflection in the year 2002 being declared as the International Year of Eco-Tourism by the United Nations. It is refreshing to see the reassurance of the Secretary-General of the World Tourism Organization in connection with his message for the International Year of Eco-Tourism in 2002 that the development of new technologies is not in contradiction with the protection of nature. Technology, nature and mankind cannot be dissociated from tourism and technology. In fact, they can be controlled to aid and advance the cause of sustainable tourism development.

These concerns were comprehensively expressed in the Earth Summit. The very broad parameters of the issues of sustainable development have been aptly summarised in the Earth Summit as "in essence sustainable development is a process of change in which the exploitation of resources, the direction of investments, the orientation of technological developments and institutional change are all in harmony and enhance both current and future potential to meet human needs and aspirations." The Agenda 21 that follows, elaborates on a large number of issues like -

– balancing between development needs and environmental requirements for present and future;

– making environmental concern part of developmental issues;

– renewal and growth of the national resources;

– reducing unsustainable pattern of production and consumption;

– participation of concerned citizens; and so on.

Any attempt to define the concept of sustainable development may be self-defeating because it may leave out more than it covers. Till date, the principles explained in the Brundtland Report (*Our Common Future*) remain the guiding and most comprehensive exposition of the concept of sustainable development – "development that meets the needs of the present without compromising the ability of future generations to meet their own needs." Quite often, crusaders for sustainable development in their zeal to pursue the concern do so without relating it to the specific realities of a specific situation. The concept of growth and development are not inimical to the concerns of sustainable development. Rather, pursuit of a balanced development is at the core of the sustainable development issues. Only uncontrolled growth which fritters away vast resources for present economic gain without concern for the future requirement is in conflict with the principles of sustainable development. Globally, the sustainable development concerns have also found reflection in a desire to have more equitable growth with social justice. However, global concern and global action for sustainable development needs to be sensitively dovetailed to the more pressing concerns of hunger and poverty. In many countries which are placed economically at a disadvantage by the process of evolution of economic history itself, the debate for future preservation seems academic to the people in their struggle for present survival.

Tourism, in such a situation can play a very positive role. As pointed out by Mr.Frangialli[22], Secretary-General of the WTO, sustainable tourism development is both positive and necessary because of three main reasons.

Firstly, travel and tourism promotes awareness about environmental issues.

Secondly, well-managed tourism is a key concern of the environment.

Thirdly, tourism itself depends on a high quality of the environment and the eco-systems.

Across the globe, there are numerous examples of unimaginative tourism development adversely affecting the environment, culture and heritage. There are also numerous examples of tourism helping to preserve threatened eco-systems and contributing to the revival of art, culture and craft. Naisbitt[23] again has referred to some good examples of positive tourism. In Rwanda, the Government was under strong pressure to cut the forest habitat of the mountain guerrillas to make way for crops and cattle movement. Sensitive management has provided the people alternative and primary source of income from eco-tourism keeping the forest habitat intact without disturbing the environment. Kenyans say "Wildlife pays, so wildlife stays". In many countries, sustainable eco-tourism is providing an alternative to unsustainable farming. In the Gulf of St. Lawrence, killing of baby seals to make trendy garments made headlines in the late 70s. Imaginative eco-tourism projects preserved the baby seals and provided a much larger income to the local population from tourists who come to watch the seals. Concern for sustainable development has manifested in some form or the other since time immemorial and cannot be said to be the preserve of the Twentieth Century only. But, an attempt to formulate a common global action on the issue started, as mentioned, in 1987 with the Brundtland Report on "Our Common Future". Surprisingly, notwithstanding the possible positive or negative impact of tourism, tourism did not find any worthwhile mention in the Report. Agenda 21 rectifies this glaring omission with a specific reference to tourism.

Irrespective of whether it is mentioned in the reports of international agencies or not, the ground realities can hardly ignore the impact of the movement of 700 million international tourists which is projected to grow to a staggering figure of 1.6 billion by 2020. If we add the number of domestic tourists, which is very large in many countries, we can visualise the great impact of tourism. For example, in India 175 m. domestic tourists and an equally large number of piligrim tourists compared to a small number of 2.6 m. international tourists greatly influence the socio-cultural environment. Sustainable tourism must, therefore, be the core concern of the Government, the industry and above all, the people.

Fortunately, such concerns have gone beyond the academic interests to formulation of action plans. Agenda 21 itself is a fairly exhaustive agenda for action. People around the world either individually or as members of concerned groups have taken up such action plans for implementation. One such attempt has resulted in the document "Beyond the Green Horizon" brought out by Worldwide Fund for Nature (WWF), U.K. and 'Tourism Concern'. The main issues of sustainable tourism have been summarised into areas of action as follows:-

1. Using resources sustainably
2. Reducing over-consumption and waste
3. Maintaining diversity
4. Integrating tourism into planning
5. Supporting local economies
6. Involving local communities
7. Consulting stakeholders and the public
8. Training staff involved in sustainable tourism projects
9. Marketing tourism responsibly
10. Undertaking research on environmental/ ecological issues related to tourism.

All these issues are self-explanatory and need no elaboration. The concept of sustainable use of resources – natural, cultural and human – is receiving increasing acceptance in principle around the world but the inner conflict of actual implementation largely remains. Used in the narrower sense of environmental protection, it would mean attempt to ensure that the non-renewable environmental assets are not irreversibly damaged. In this objective, tourism can be a positive force. The BBC Report of 1992 (The Natural World Portrait of the Planet, BBC II, 23rd Feb. 1992) reported that there are about 5000 national parks and wildlife sanctuaries designed to be tourist attractions which provide protection and preservation to flora and fauna. More and more countries have clearly and prominently put the objective of sustainable development in the forefront of their tourism policy. The Report "Beyond the Green Horizon" refers to the Tourism Authority of Thailand, the mission statement of the Wales Tourist Board, the English Tourist Board, the New Zealand Tourism Policy, all of which speak forcefully about sustainable development. The nations of the world, through the mouthpiece of the World Tourism Organization, have again and again declared their honest intentions for sustainable development and have pledged to work towards achieving the objective. The Bali Declaration of the WTO states: "Tourism development is to be carried out on the basis of careful planning with the broad involvement and active participation of local communities, including women and the young generation, and the private sector to balance economic, social, cultural and religious values and environmental conservation so that sustainable development is achieved".[24]

In the Male Declaration, the participants of the Asia Pacific Ministers' Conference on Tourism and Environment pledged continuing support for the vision and goals of a sustainable future, as conceived and articulated in the 1987 Brundtland Commission Report, the 1992 Earth Summit, the Rio Declaration and Agenda 21. These concerns were further extended to the tourism industry through subsequent efforts such as Agenda 21 for the Travel and Tourism Industry, the World Conference on Sustainable Tourism, and the 1996 International Conference on Tourism and Heritage Management, encompassing the following precepts:

* fostering awareness of environmental ethics in tourism among communities and consumers;
* conservation and sustainable use of resources;
* public guardianship of the natural environment;
* reducing consumption and waste;
* natural, social and cultural diversity;
* integrated tourism planning for sustainability;
* support for local economies;
* local community involvement;
* consulting tourism stakeholders and the public;
* human resource development;

* responsible tourism marketing;
* ongoing inquiry into sustainability issues;
* measurements to monitor tourism's impacts on environment, culture and heritage; and
* use of environmental impact assessments in tourism planning.

The Manila Declaration of 1997 on the Social Impact of Tourism is devoted entirely to the various social implications of tourism development.

The discussion paper "Beyond the Green Horizon" points out that there are growing and glaring instances of negative impact of tourism which is not properly planned. It gives a few examples of–

- coastal resorts developed in Thailand where the waters of Gulf of Thailand no longer support shellfish;
- beach pollution in Philippines because of unregulated constructions;
- Nepal - where waste and litter left by trekkers and mountaineers have created pollution in the snow areas affecting mountain;
- many tourist destinations in Indonesia, in the French Pyrenees in the Mediterranean affected by pollution waste and sewage problems –created by huge movement of tourist;

the "loved to death" tendency of ecological damage in most national parks caused by enthusiastic tourists beyond the absorbing capacity of the place.

Such invasion of tourism also has the potentiality of affecting the lifestyle and culture of smaller communities, for example, in small island resorts or in hundreds of special cultural destinations away from the metropolis. There are innumerable instances of tourism providing the only source of income and employment to such small local communities, and also of cultural heritage on the verge of decay being revived and being made a source of income through tourism. There are equally large number of instances of people being re-located, communities losing traditional means of livelihood because of growth of tourism. "Beyond the Green Horizon" refers to beach tourism development uprooting the fishing communities in Penang, golf course construction throwing out communities living for generations in Hana, Maui, Maunawili and Waianae in Hawaii.

Over-consumption of natural and other resources in the tourism industry is another major concern globally but particularly in areas where shortage of such resources creates severe tension between the industry and the local population.

Quite often, people suffering from lack of civic amenities are affected further due to patronage to tourism requirements and the mismatch between demand and supply often results in unsustainable over-exploitation. Reducing consumption and wastages in the industry is no longer just a slogan but a necessary requirement for the future development of the industry. The nature of this problem was examined in relation to Ladakh in "Indian Tourism Beyond the Millennium" and the experience is worth recapitulating.

"Any tourism development plan has to be concerned about providing such basic facilities. In a situation like that of Ladakh, with perennial shortage of civic amenities, tourism development may have immediately two-fold effect. First, it will put further pressure on the already stressed infrastructure. As over-crowding occurs, the host community may find itself under greater pressure from visitors, a pressure which may change the rhythms of a community's lifestyle. It causes irritation to the local public and this sense of irritation runs through prominently in all the discussions on Leh referred to earlier. Secondly, such irritation aggravates when priority is given to the needs of the tourists, giving rise to what Jenkins calls 'irridex effect'. In such a situation, often solution is sought in trying to determine, what is generally called the 'carrying capacity' of the product and attempting to regulate the number of tourists. Such an attempt in fact is a recognition of the existence of a conflict between the temptation that tourism offers for maximum commercial exploitation and the need for preserving such heritage for future generation. Basically, it is a question of balancing present economic gains with long-term interest of future sustainability. It is not surprising that the Seminar on 'Tourism and Environment' held in Leh (17th-18th September, 1995) thus recommended –

> "There is an urgent need to fix a ceiling for tourist traffic to the area. Steps should be taken to fix an upper ceiling of 25-30 thousand tourists per year so that the traffic is related with the existing carry ing capacity, human and material resources and availability of supplies."

It is also interesting to note that the UNESCO Workshop on Sustainable Tourism Development in World Heritage Sites – 'Planning for Hue' has the following basic overriding recommendation which amplifies the general conflict between tourism development and sustainable needs:-

> "Over-arching all of the specific recommen-dations... is the general observation that the overwhelming majority of the participants felt that the projected target of 10,00,000 tourists per year by the year 2000 is far too high to be realistic, manageable or sustainable. Such a number may well exceed the carrying capacity of the monuments and also the capacity of the infrastructure." The resolution goes on to explain the possible effects on infrastructure and environment and emphasizes the need for pursuing quality of tourists rather than quantity."

Diversity - natural, cultural, social - is a motivating factor for tourism and in fact, the very fabric of tourism growth in the future. The future challenge in tourism lies primarily in maintaining this diversity as an asset while ensuring that mass movement of tourism creating a global village does not deprive the industry of its most sustainable reason for travel. In many ways, globalisation is both a bane and a blessing to tourism. The study on Ladakh again draws attention to some of the socio-cultural problems of sustainability of tourism that every small region faces. As tourism grew in Ladakh, attracted by the diversity of the landscape, the unique ethnic tradition, and the cultural treasure of the old monasteries, the process of urbanisation also started. Tourism became the predominant culture uprooting people from rural settings to tourist places and in the process depriving the cultural heritage, of the primary source of its sustenance, the loving care of the people. This conflict also has been analysed in the context of Ladakh. "Such cultural conflict has another dimension which is also relevant to Ladakh. Most of the heritage sites are in rural pastoral settings sustained by the community ethos of an agricultural community with deep cultural moorings in the heritage around them. Such heritage grew with their tender care and craftsmanship. Change and development have affected these rural attachments and social commitments to the heritage. The Public Hearing in Ladakh and in particular the lead paper of Helena Norberg-Hodge and Janet Rizvi pointed out that development has changed the agricultural system and social structures in Ladakh. With the shift in economic power to the urban areas, rural-based heritage has lost the nucleus of support system, and starved of such support, heritage management has of necessity had to make compromises on commercial considerations. Development of heritage tourism itself for such products, located in rural areas presents some inherent problems. Boniface and Fowler put the problem succinctly – "how is it best to present a rural attraction to an audience largely soaked in urban life way?...how can the essential rural nature of a countryside be preserved when tourist needs require the trapping of suburbia or town centre–large parks for cars... cafes and convenience, good access roads ...?"[25]

Such process of urbanisation affecting the socio-cultural diversity leading to emergence of what is being called 'monoculture' brings in other problems of urbanisation – the change in lifestyle, erosion of traditional values and the tendency of the younger generation to imitate the opulent looking exciting lifestyle of an alien culture. In the same manner, traditional culture, the main attraction for tourists, when it becomes a 'product to be sold to the tourists' loses the conspicuous attraction of uniqueness and authenticity. Keeping a balance between the two is one of the most important challenges of tourism development.

The entire basis of the concept of sustainable development is integration of economic needs, social requirements and cultural values for the present and for the future. They are concerns cutting across sectors. Without integration and coordination, such concerns cannot ever be properly addressed or effectively handled. Tourism, as it is, requires coordination, of many different activities. Yet, surprisingly as in India, in most countries its planning and development is not integrated into the socio-economic planning process of the country. The general tendency to concentrate on short-term economic gains leading to over-exploitation of resources in the tourism sector can be countered only if viable economic alternatives are provided. Integrated planning may provide such alternatives by way of development of arts and craft, industry based on local skills which again can be means of enhancing the quality of tourism attraction.

"Beyond the Green Horizon" invites attention to an inconspicuous but important problem that may arise in the absence of integrated planning. Tourism being product specific, is often promoted on the basis of competitive advantage of a place. Therefore, promotion of tourism can cause regional and social disparities leading to social tension and hostility.

Naturally, what needs to be done is wide and difficult. The basic problem is of balance between the present needs of survival and sensitivity to the future requirements. But foresight which encourages taking action for the future is often blunted by the struggle for present economic well-being. The action plans for sustainable tourism development will, therefore, require more of awareness of people and their willingness to adopt them rather than force of legislation. In India, it is reported, that the entire arena of sustainable development issues is covered by more than 70 legislations and official guidelines. Sometimes, such codal requirements in fact only create impediments for well-intended schemes. Imaginative implementation, therefore, is the primary need.

The United Nations Economic and Social Council and the Commission on Sustainable Development in the 7th Session from 19th-30th April, 1999 discussed a large number of issues on tourism and sustainable development. All these issues could be basically grouped into four areas –

(1) Identifying the role of the stakeholders – the Government, the industry and the people and to create partnership among them for outlining the action programme.

(2) Participation of the community in the process of sustainable development and their active role.

(3) Creating awareness among all the players, among the people who are likely to be affected, among tourists and many host communities about respective roles and responsibilities.

(4) Institutional and legal framework which takes care of the special problems of specific areas and are integrated into the socio-economic system.

On each of these areas, specific action required to be taken are numerous, diverse and complex, and, therefore, not attempted to be elaborated here.

Creating awareness can be part of the national policy for environmental education, particularly for those who have to implement the various provisions of sustainable development, and training of those who come into contact peripherally with tourists e.g. the guides and tour operators. 'Awareness creation' also requires an effort on the part of the Government for constant monitoring of the environmental impact of tourism and sharing those results with tne public. The industry needs to develop energy saving-waste reducing technology, recycling of non-renewable resources. The industry also can adopt green practices and own responsibility to give part of the benefit to the community for integrated development of green practices. The wider issues of sustainability continuously throw up difficult problems. Therefore, problem solving research and technological development for conflict resolution is also an important requirement of sustainable development policy.

It is at this stage, pertinent to make a difference between 'eco-tourism', 'sustainable development' and 'sustainable tourism'. We have already explained the basic tenets of sustainable development. Sustainable tourism is that part of tourism which conforms to those concerns of sustainable development. The principles of sustainable tourism development were defined by the World Tourism Organization in 1988. Sustainable tourism is "envisaged as leading to management of all resources in such a way that economic, social and aesthetic needs can be fulfilled while maintaining cultural integrity, essential ecological processes, biological diversity and life-support systems". Eco-tourism is again difficult to define. Much has been written but definition has always the pitfall of saying too much or too little. The easier option is to describe its commonly accepted characteristcs –

- environmentally responsible travel for visitor and local people
- tourism that is nature-based
- main motivation is enjoyment and appreciation of nature

- generally confined to small groups, specially arranged and not mass tourism

- has low adverse visitor impact

- promotes conservation by generating economic benefits to local people.

The difference between the two concepts is obvious. Sustainable development covers much wider concerns than just eco-tourism. It is also obvious that eco-tourism efforts cannot survive in isolation and have, therefore, to be integrated into the overall planning of sustainable tourism development.

Human Resource Development

The importance of Human Resource Development crops up in any discussion of tourism whether it is in relation to impact of information technology or in relation to sustainable development. As we have noted, some of the implications of the paradigm shift in the content and quality of tourism are obvious. As Dr.Eduardo Fayos-Sola[26] has pointed out, that the customer is individualised. This is also a fall out, to some extent, of the segmentation of the market as we have seen resulting from all the new emerging influences. In an interesting analysis, Joseph Pine and James Gilmore (The Experience Economy, Harvard Business School, Central Press, 1999) have referred to a syndrome described as the concept of "experience economy" which is changing the tourism scenario. More travellers now desire to make their travel a memorable or novel experience. Market economy is adapting to tourist demand by using services as the cutting-edge tool and goods as the props to engage and attract individual customers in such a way as to create a memorable experience. The arrival of or travel to an "experience economy" means that the product is being sold and consumed. It also means that supply would mean moving from provision of a service to creating an experience. Such experience being essentially personal and individualised, transition to experience economy is linked to the trend of the individualised customer. The strategy of human resource development in such a scenario, therefore, will have to reposition itself to train individuals to service this experience.

In a globalised context, the markets are becoming increasingly competitive. Flexibility of services, capability to take to new technology and new demands, therefore, provide the competitive edge. In the new age of tourism, influence of information technology has been over-powering and all encompassing. But, in the last resort, technology is as good as the man behind it. It is significant that Goh Chok Tong, the Prime Minister of Singapore - the market savvy, technology driven City State – in his 1997 National Day Speech said "In the information age, human talent, not physical resources or financial capital, is the key factor for economic competitiveness and success". In an age which is flooded with information available at the fingertips, intelligent use of information provides power and not just the availability of information as such. One is almost reminded of Eliot's lament long back "where is the knowledge we have lost in information. Where is the wisdom we have lost in knowledge".

Human resource development that provides input to the information technology enables the service provider to adopt the requirements of information technology and will, therefore, be a major requirement of the future tourism development. Eduardo Fayol-Sola[27] has drawn attention to another interesting factor as to why human resource will be of crucial importance in the future. As access to technology itself has become increasingly democratic, information and technology will be widely known and shared. Therefore, there will be no great advantage in having technology itself which is known and available to everyone. The competitive advantage will be provided only by the quality of the human resource which uses the technology. In the 21st Century, the develoment of technology being, as we have seen, fast paced, the key challenge will not be just providing tourism education but in having a system of education that is capable of imparting strategic skills that enable human material to adapt to fast-changing requirements. Eduardo Fayol-Sola calls it the DNA of tourism organization. It follows naturally that in the planning of human resource development, quality should be the uppermost concern. But, even the best-managed human resource development programmes may not be able to directly touch all the players who need to be trained. In most countries, resource constraint will leave out of the training system the most important segments – the NGOs, local governments and the local service providers. Training of trainers to achieve a wider coverage with multiplier effect will, therefore, be a primary requirement. Management of change should be, therefore, an important input in the training process.

In India, for example, the human resource development output touches only the fringe of the demand and that too is confined to servicing the star-category hotels. Thousands of hotels and restaurants servicing 175 million domestic tourists do not benefit from the service upgradation that human resource development brings. To spread the concept of 'quality in service' to wider areas, it is essential to include these small but key players as well. Considering the mismatch between the demand and supply and the cost and time involved in getting formal education for all those huge numbers involved in the tourism sector, the only possible way in India to expand this area is to embark on a policy of 'Training of Trainers'. It is also essential to create quality consciousness among the industry and also among the customers.

Tourism education has also to be seen in a wider context. If education is to be strategic, it must respond to multi-cultural sensitivity and should be capable of adjustment to local varieties and requirement.

The context of human resource development edcuation also is getting wider in most countries. With huge numbers of tourists descending on a tourist place, naturally many problems of cultural conflicts and environmental pressures arise. Both the visitors and the host communities need to be properly oriented to such preserse so that the adverse impact is minimised. The scope of human resource development education, therefore, will have to extend to destination management in all its entirety.

Globalisation and Tourism

How does the globalisation and liberalisation process of the 21st century affect tourism? We have seen how spread of technology, economic libralisation and mass tourism have made the world a global village. We have also seen there are many pitfalls of insensitive of development. The World Tourism Organization has pointed out three main issues that need to be kept in view in the liberalised scenario.

First, that liberalisation should be tempered with the need for sustainable development. Therefore, while tourism industry shares the urge for liberalisation with other industries, and grows together, it should be controlled liberalisation consistent with the global ethical concern. The Global Code of Ethics of the World Tourism Organisation (WTO) (Appendix-III) call for liberalisation to optimise the beneficial effect of creation of income and employment through tourism.

Second, the impact of liberalisation on tourism needs to be very closely studied. There are feelings that developing countries are getting less than they can get from tourism because of leakages in the system. The developed countries are also not benefitting as much as they should because of incomplete liberalisation and the consumers are not getting the benefit from all the productivity gains brought in by technology and globalisation as they are entitled to expect.

Third, as pointed out earlier, neglect of tourism within the globalised systems of the United Nations while addressing the issues of sustainable development is depriving tourism of the needed focus to achieve balanced growth. It is universally acknowledged that the process of liberalisation must not affect local employment. Liberalisation should be so guided that local skill is upgraded rather than being replaced by more skilful ones from outside. The process of liberalisation must also recognize cultural heritage and uniqueness of each place. Strength and variety and not homogenity holds the key to the future of tourism.

Against this backdrop of the general issues influencing the growth of global tourism, it would be appropriate to briefly analyse the Indian tourism scenario. That a country endowed with such potential and variety should languish with only 2.7 million foreign tourist arrivals is always a puzzle. But, on the positive side, it also implies that India can look forward to a brighter situation in the coming days if the challenges for development are tackled with a sense of purpose and determination. Peter Drucker's observation that "long-range planning does not deal with future decisions but with the future of present decisions" appears to be very relevant for India.

One special feature of Indian tourism scenario is the huge number of domestic tourism and its rapid growth. The issues relating to sustainability become even more pertinent in this scenario. The tremendous growth of domestic tourism to 176 million in 2000 puts additional pressure on both the inadequate infrastructure and the fragile eco-system. The small number of foreign tourist arrivals should not create a false sense of complacency about sustainable tourism issues.

The present scenario of tourism in India can be summed up in 3 broad parameters. First, that India has tremendous potentials which are not yet fully achieved. Second, that the future of tourism in India looks extremely optimistic but realisation of that optimism will depend on removal of a large number of small impediments. The future action plan should be based on realistic assessment of these impediments. Third, in a competitive global environment, we also need to adopt new strategies to be able to meet the future challenges.

India's progress in tourism growth from 1950 seen in isolation may not look too bad. From 17,000 arrivals and Rs.7.7 crores in foreign exchange earnings to the present position of 2.67 million arrivals and over Rs.14,000 crores in earnings does look good at the first glance. Even around the 80s, India's position was much better than many of the competing countries today but the arrivals of many countries and particularly many small neighbours in South-East Asia who are competing with us in the last two decades have been much better. The table below gives a comparative position of arrivals and earnings as well as the global rank of China, Thailand, Singapore, Indonesia, Malaysia and India which makes this point abundantly clear: India's position globally both in arrivals and earnings have remained almost constant primarily because other countries have moved even faster.

	1980 Arrivals (m)	Rank	Share	1997 Arrivals (m)	Rank	Share
China	3.5	18	1.22	23.7	06	3.89
Thailand	1.8	27	0.65	7.2	20	1.18
Singapore	2.5	22	0.90	6.5	22	1.07
Indonesia	0.5	58	0.18	5.1	27	0.85
Malaysia	2.1	25	0.74	6.2	23	1.02
India	1.2	44	0.42	2.37	44	0.39

The table also shows that during this period India's share in the world market slipped even further because other countries have taken away that market share. [27]

Two factors appear significant in this context. First, that there is increasing competition in the world for the market share and number of countries which have more than 1 million arrivals have increased from 15 in 1950 to 70 in 1999. Second, India's growth rate has also been slower than the competing destinations even though at some points it has been higher than the world average in recent times. The following table shows India's inadequate growth rate during these two decades compared to the other competing destinations[29].

Average annual growth rate 1980-1997	
World	04.56
China	11.93
Thailand	08.31
Singapore	05.66
Malaysia	06.57
Indonesia	14.40
India	04.13

Growth of Indonesia (from 0.5 m to 5.1 m), Turkey (from 0.9 m to 9 m), South Africa (from 0.7 m to 5.4 m), only highlight the intensity of competition as also the possibility of equal growth for India if determined and positive policies are followed.

Both the World Travel & Tourism Council and the World Tourism Organization have made very optimistic projections about India's future growth. According to the WTO, between 2000-2010, the growth rate of India will be around 6.5% which is much higher than the world average. WTO in its "2020 Vision" has estimated India's future growth as follows:

Actual	Forecasts		Growth Rates (% p.a.)		
1995	2010	2020	1995-2020	2000-2010	2010-2020
2,124	5,089	8900	5.9	6.5	5.8

India will retain the predominant position within South Asia with 8.9 million arrivals by 2010 out of a total of 18.75 million. This will give India a market share of 47.4% in the South Asia region. Though predominant, however, this market share will be smaller than what it is at present primarily because the other neighbours are also expected to make good progress in the meantime.

Even with such optimistic growth, South Asia's share will be only 1.1% of the total global arrivals. There will still be a lot to catch up with competitors near home like China, Malaysia, Thailand, etc. However, WTTC's study entitled 'India - The Tourism Imperative' shows that between 2001-2011 in some key parameters,

India's growth is expected to be, in fact, much higher than the world average[30].

	INDIA	CHINA	THAILAND	MALAYSIA	SINGAPORE	WORLD
TRAVEL & TOURISM INDUSTRY GDP (US$m)						
Real growth between 2001-2011 (% annualized)	10.0(1)	9.0(3)	7.5(9)	6.1(20)	6.7(14)	3.3
TRAVEL & TOURISM ECONOMY GDP (US$m)						
Real growth Between 2001-2011 (% annualized)	9.1(3)	8.8(4)	7.2(10)	5.9(25)	6.8(13)	3.6
TRAVEL & TOURISM EMPLOYMENT GDP (US$000)						
Real growth between 2001-2011 (% annualized)	3.6(41)	2.0(101)	3.0(62)	3.5(47)	3.2(55)	2.4
TRAVEL & TOURISM ECONOMY EMPLOYMENT GDP						
Real growth Between 2001-2011 (% annualized)	2.8(73)	1.8(113)	2.8(70)	3.3(50)	3.3(49)	2.3

Obviously such projections will materialise only if identified action to achieve them are in position. We had earlier referred to the broad agenda action identified by WTTC. Mr.Geoffrey H. Lipman, the then President of the World Travel & Tourism Council in his Oberoi Foundation Lecture in New Delhi in January 1999 summed up the potential of Indian tourism economy which could achieve by 2020 the following landmarks -

6.6% of GDP - a 1% increase and a jump to Rs. 5,00,000 Crore

6.8% of employment - again a 1% increase and 8 million new Jobs

7.6% of capital investment - 1.2% increase and a jump to Rs. 1,30,000 Crore

12% of exports - again a 1.2% increase and a jump to Rs. 1,60,000 Crore.

He also summed up the five-point agenda of action if the country was to move towards achieving these objectives -

i) to make travel and tourism a strategic economic priority;

ii) to pursue open and competitive markets;

iii) to pursue policy of sustainable development; and

iv) to remove some fundamental barriers to growth - infrastructure deficiencies: high taxes and in adequate service skills.

In August 2001, based on its preliminary surveys using the Tourism Satellite Account methodology, the WTTC India Initiative published 'The Tourism Imperative' which identified very impressive contribution of tourism to the economy of India and outlined the future policy action. Mr. Jean-Claude Baumgarten, President of WTTC in his open letter to the Tourism Minister has identified the following to be addressed with urgency and resolve to establish a stable foundation for tourism, in India -

- Augment airline seat availability
- Simplify visa procedures
- Privatize the existing airports
- Correct India's image
- Open more international airports
- Upgrade basic tourist facilities
- Evolve uniform taxation systems conducive to tourism
- Leverage private sector funds and skills . to maintain and market India's heritage
- Market a single ticket for all national heritage sites
- Open up the accommodations sectors.

It is refreshing to note that the Ministry of Tourism is alive to the challenges and are aware of the urgent need to take concreate action. The action progamme drawn up by the hospitality industry at the instance of the Government is exhaustive and revealing (Appendix-IV). It clearly lays down the road map for action. It is now a time for action.

A recent survey by A. T. Kearny has indentified the infrastructural gaps in India as perceived by foreign tourists:

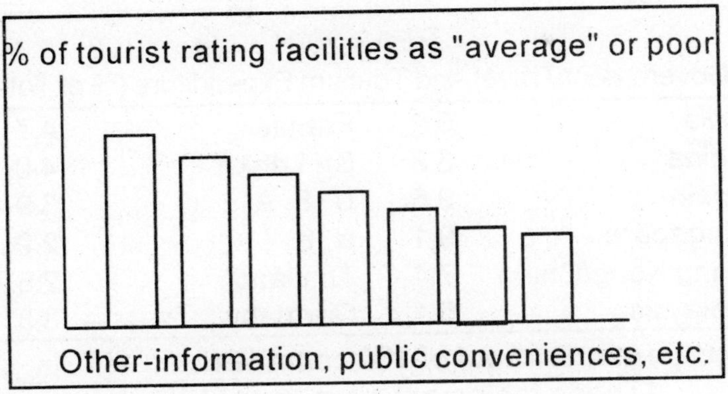

India is also on comparatively weak grounds in respect of many basic infrastructure facilities like accommodation.

	'000 Rooms	1990-98 (CAGR)%
China	765	20
Thailand	279	08
Indonesia	232	10
Malaysia	108	17
India	067	06

In such a situation, as repeatedly mentioned, we need a strong public-private initiative and a big push from the Government. Unfortunately, the policy pronouncements of the Government contained in the Five Year Plan documents and the yearly budget statements do not reflect that the sector has gained

Government expenditure on tourism as percentage of the total expenditure, India ranks 153 out of 160 countries. The following table shows how poorly we fare compared to some big destinations:

YEAR 2001

Government Travel And Tourism Expenditure (% of Total)

India	0.9	France	4.7
China	3.8	Sri Lanka	4.0
Spain	9.5	U. S. A.	3.9
Singapore	9.1	U. K.	2.9
Hong Kong/China	7.4	Thailand	2.6
Malaysia	5.1	Germany	3.3

India ranks 153rd out of 160 countries.

(These tables are from unpublished document of Government of India, Ministry of Tourism, titled 'Tourism in India - Opportunities and Constraints')

Apart from such generic issues, some more specific issues of marketing mentioned below also need attention in the context of changing global situations -

(a) There is need for a new market strategy which must be driven by new technology and which is in tune with the consumer demands. Such strategy must address the micro issues, moving away from the preoccupation with macro dimensions.

(b) India's continuing dependence on long-haul markets has to be reassessed. Strategy for alternative development of shorter-haul arrivals from East Asia and the Pacific regions because of the compulsions of consumers choice should get priority attention.

(c) To overcome the disadvantages of distance from primary outbound markets, India will have to offer incentives better than given by others. Major incentives could be by way of ease of travel, availability of easy air seats, removal of hassles of getting a visa, etc. There is a widespread feeling that all these factors act as major impediments at present. Reportedly there is excess air seat capacity to and from India, yet it is often reported by the travel industry that getting a seat in some sectors at some periods of time can be a major hassle.

(d) The general impression among tourists is that India's attractions far exceed their expectations but visitors, experiences are often less than expected. No tourist could expect the home situation to be replicated in India but he would naturally expect a warm and traditional welcome which the long tradition of culture and civilization of India should normally ensure. As it is often said, one does not get a second chance to make a first impression. The tourist must find India as a place to relax and enjoy his/her holiday without hassles. A tourism-friendly culture has to be recreated.

Naturally, the potentials are very great and the challenges are daunting. The responses have to be adequate and, therefore, the list of things to be done will tend to get longer and longer. implementation is the guiding need of the hour. Albert Camus' advice in a different context is relevant to Indian tourism - "I shall tell you a great secret, my friend. Don't wait for the last judgement; it takes place everyday".

Reference

1. W.T.O: The Economic Impact of Tourism, undated Brochure.
2. John Naisbitt: Global Paradox. William Morrow and Company, New York 1994. p 104.
3. WTO : The Economic Impact of Tourism, undated Brochure.
4. WTO : Tourism 2020 Vision, Executive Summary June 1998, p. 4.
5. WTO : Tourism 2020 vision, Executive Summary 1998, p. 30.
6. WTO : Tourism to the year 2000, Madrid 1991, p. 7
7. John Naisbitt, op. Cit., p. 21, 24, 30.
8. Ibid, p. 23.
9. WTO : Tourism 2020 Vision: Executive Summary 1998. p. 3.
10. Ibid, p. 3.
11. WTO: Tourism 2020 Vision: Executive Summary 1998. p. 35.
12. Naisbitt: op.cit. p.122.
13. Time: June 16, 1997. p. 46.
14. WTO: Tourism to the Year 2000. Madrid. 1991. p.10
15. Time. op.cit. p. 43.
16. WTO. Tourism 2020 Vision: Executive Summary. 1998. Madrid.
17. Naisbitt. op.cit. p. 95.
18. Naisbitt: op.cit p. 80.
19. WTO: Vision 2020: Executive Summary. 1998. Madrid. p. 36-37.
20. WTO: Tourism to the Year 2000. Madrid. p.20-21.
21. Lord Marshall of Knightsbridge: Som Nath Chib Memorial Lecture – The Role of Civil Aviation in promoting Tourism in the 21st Century. International Fellowship Foundation of India, New Delhi. 1999. p.23.
22. Mr. Francesco Frangialli, Secretary General, WTO: Observations on International Tourism. p. 27.

23. Naisbitt. op.cit. p.128-129.
24. M.P. Bezbaruah: Indian Tourism Beyond the Millennium- Gyan Publishing House, New Delhi. 2000- p 205.
25. ibid, p. 60.
26. Dr Eduardo Fayos-Sola: in Tourism Challenges in the 21st Century. Human Resource Development in the Asia and the Pacific. WTO Madrid. 2000. p.17.
27. Dr.Eduardo Fayol-Sola. op. cit. p.19.
28. W. T. O.: Yearbook of Tourism Statistics Vol. 1. 1999. Madrid. p. 13.
29. W. T. O. Yearbook of Tourism Statistics Vol. 1. 1999. Madrid p.13.
30. WTTC: India - The Tourism Imperative. August. 2001.

2

MEASURING THE ECONOMIC IMPACT OF TOURISM

"Then you should say what you mean"
the march Hare went on.

"I do" Alice hastily replied; "at least – at least I mean what I say – that's the same thing, you know."

"Not the same thing a bit!" said the Hatter. "Why, you might just as well say that 'I see what I eat is the same thing as I eat what I see'!"

Lewis Carroll, "Alice's Adventures in Wonderland"

The story of the growth of tourism and its emergence as the biggest industry of the world has been discussed in the previous Chapter. The factors that will shape the nature of tourism in future also have been analysed. Inspite of such tremendous potential unfortunately, tourism does not always find the pride of place in the socio-economic planning of many countries

It is true that the importance of tourism in socio-economic development of nations has been recognised in general but the actual impact has not always been apparent. Even the tremendous growth of tourism since the 80s as already recounted left out many areas from the benefits of such growth either from lack of initiative or from lack of awareness. The United Nations and the World Tourism Organization had been for some time working on devising an accounting procedure where the economic impact of tourism would be clearly brought out. Continuing this initiative, in 1999 the World Tourism Organization organised an international conference in Nice, France to discuss ways of implementing what has now come to be known as the 'Tourism Satellite Account' (TSA). The process was started more than a decade back and, therefore, the Secretary-General in his address compared the conference to the finishing line of a stage race. In May 2000 in Vancouver, Canada, another international conference reviewed the progress so far made and adopted modalities of carrying it forward.

Many countries around the world are, however, only waking up to the concept and are asking the basic questions. Why is it needed? What does it do? Is not tourism's contribution otherwise also well known?

As we have seen, the figures of growth and general figures of contribution are well known. Growth of tourism arrivals from 70 million in 1960 to 700 million in 2000 and of receipts from $6.9 billion to 476 billion during the same period is awe-inspiring. It is well-known that it is the biggest industry of the 21st Century, in terms of contribution to GDP, employment generation, share in exports etc., it has no equal. It has surpassed industries like petrochemicals, automobiles and others in terms of its output. In a span of 20 years, tourism has grown almost ten times keeping in tune with the projection of the WTO that by

2020, the international arrivals will reach 1.6 billion. As Naisbitt concludes[1] "as the world economy integrates and the global society becomes increasingly homogeneous, the needs of individuals to retain a sense of self in a sea of homogenization grows stronger. Consequently, people are more likely, not less likely to travel...."

This growth of tourism has been propelled by many factors which have been discussed in the previous Chapter. The future, in fact, is even more impressive and in all likelihood, would surpass the estimates of WTO. It is known that the present growth has been possible with only about 7 percent of the population of the world capable of travelling actually travelling.

In economic terms, international tourism receipts are classified as 'exports' and international tourism expenditure as 'imports'. For many countries, international tourism is an indispensable source of foreign earnings. According to a WTO Report, tourism is one of the 5 top export categories for 83 percent of the countries and the main source of the foreign currency earnings for at least 38 percent of them. It is reported that tourism contributes from 30-70 percent of the GDP of many Caribbean countries.

In 1998, international tourism and international fare receipts (receipts related to passenger transport and residence of other countries) accounted for roughly 8 percent of total export earnings on goods and services world-wide. Total international tourism receipts including those generated by international fares amounted to an estimated $533 billion surpassing all other international trade categories.

Such impressive performance should be of particular interest to the developing and the underdeveloped countries because of the various socio-economic impact of tourism. In the Caribbean, for example, tourism accounts for 50 to 70 percent of the economy of each of the States. The benefits of tourism are generally acknowledged and well perceived. It creates jobs and income; disperse effects widely; spread social harmony and understanding, allows use of local resources and is not dependent on heavy outside capital investment; and offers infinite varieties and possibilities. Using Walt Disney's metaphor we can say that "as long as something is left in human imagination, tourism will have scope to grow". The Mexican experience beautifully narrated by Antonio Savignac, former Secretary General of WTO and former Planning Minister of Mexico in his National Tourism Day lecture in India can again be repeated.

"A strange beast that seemed to grow like a weed, with no fertilizer, irrigation, care or attention......

Our conclusions were surprising at least to us, who were novices in this field.

1. It could be developed and promoted almost anywhere.

2. It grew with little if any government help, programs or policies.

3. It offered an infinity of products and possibilities such as business, conventions, cruise, nature (parks, lakes, mountains), archaeology, cities, sports, adventure, sun and beaches, culture, folklore, music, astronomy and so forth.

4. It was relatively free of restrictions, unlike other exports of goods and commodities which were subject to quotas, taxes, import permits and many others.

5. It generally did not consume non-renewable resources, nor did it involve dangerous processes.

6. It was labour - intensive and, being a personal service, hard to automate or replace.

7. The technology for its development was well known and easily available, with no major technological changes foreseen or any risk of premature obsolescence.

8. Training of personnel was generally easy, available and quick (except for managerial posts) with minimum requisites of previous studies or training (as opposed to high-tech industries).

9. Foreign tourism was capable of providing an ever-increasing flow of foreign currency.

10. The foreign import component of the industry was exceptionally low (excluding airplanes). It was estimated to be of only 6 to 8 percent of the total

investments, as compared to 35 to 45 percent for the automobile industry. This meant most of the investments and expenditures would remain in the country, with little foreign currency impact." ....

The list of the benefits of tourism is long. But, in the present world scenario, one of the strongest contribution could be that tourism helps transfer of resources from the rich to the poor countries and thereby helps equitable distribution of income without conflict. During the period from 1980 to 2000, international tourism more than doubled. During this period, 60 countries of the world were getting steadily poorer than what they were.[2] During the same period, the income gap between the fifth living in the richest countries and the fifth living in the poorest countries has been increasing. This is a problem to be tackled unless we want the world to go back to a world of strife and conflict, caused by economic imbalance. Promotion of tourism which can be based on the existing natural geographical and cultural resources of a country can help to minimize this growing imbalance.

Yet, tourism is not high in the agenda of most of the countries which can benefit from it. Tourism gets the pride of place neither in the national budget allocations nor in the promotional budgets nor even in the thinking process of most of the countries,

It is difficult to explain this contradiction. One of the reasons could be that a vicious cycle operates. Those countries which need tourism most do not have the resources to provide the required infrastructure and, therefore, continue to remain in the background. Since they do not have infrastructure, tourism potentials remain unrealised. In many cases, it is a question of perception. As models of development, most countries would like to go by the traditional approach of looking at industry and manufacturing or even trade, rather than tourism whose contribution in many countries like India is grouped under the heading "Invisibles". In other cases tourism is just taken for granted because as Mr. Savignac explains with the experience of Mexico tourism is a "strange beast" that seemed to grow like a weed with no fertilizer, irrigation, care or attention.

Such an attitude is not surprising because tourism is a composite multi-dimensional activity made up of many activities whose effects are inter-related but not always seen. The World Travel and Tourism Council, we have noted, has identified about 30 sub-sectors to be at the core of what we call tourism and travel activity. The number increases and the problems are compounded if we go to the periphery of activities which make tourism possible.

Another problem is that even if the activities are identified, the impact is not always direct. The impact of various tourism-related activities can be broadly grouped into four categories.

i) Initial Effects

Sometimes called 'direct effects', these trace the impact generated by a certain quantity of goods and services offered for final consumption in the sector itself and its constituents.

ii) *Primary Indirect Effects*

These effects trace the impact the given sector generates on the rest of the economy by way of intermediate consumption resulting from initial effects.

iii) *Indirect Industrial Effects*

This is the impact on the rest of the economy resulting from primary indirect effects, i.e., indirect industrial effects indicates the manner in which suppliers in the surveyed sector are affected when the given sector are affected when the given sector satisfies final consumtion demand to a given money value.

iv) *Induced Effects*

This refers to the effects of household income arising form initial and indirect primary and industrial effects, that is injected back into the economy. This reinjection in the form of household spending will, in turn, create indirect primary industrial, and induced effects.

These are some of the problems that the Tourism Satellite Account (TSA) seeks to address. Basically, TSA intends to establish a set of statistics, which are internationally compatible, well-defined and consistent. While statistics relevant for tourism sector may be available, they are submerged in broader statistics. TSA seeks to cull out the relevant statistics, fit them into the definitional and classification moulds of tourism accounts and present a set of credible numbers that are attributable to tourism.

Naturally, this statistical process should be able to reasonably take into account "the ripple effects" of the tourism activity. As Doug Fyfe said in the Somnath Chib Memorial Lecture in New Delhi, "The Tourism Satellite Account that people keep talking about is the tourism industry's balance sheet. It is an input, output, analytic framework."[3]

The basic objective of TSA has been simply put by WTO[4] as -

"Governments often underestimate the economic benefits that tourism provides because it is not as visible as industries such as manufacturing. Business enterprises often fail to realize the role tourism plays in their success and they do not take full advantage of opportunities in this rapidly growing activity because it is not measured in the same way as other productive activities are measured. And, citizens may not seriously consider job opportunities that the growing tourism industries provide because these industries are not referenced in the books, magazines and newspapers they read.

Results of the TSA will allow us to understand the true size and value of the tourism industry. Tracking the data over a period of years will allow governments to make better informed policy decisions. But, above all, the *Tourism Satellite Account* will help improve the image and stature of the industry. It will expand the influence that tourism officials and private sector businesses have with policy-makers at the highest levels of government.

The TSA does not have anything to do with outer space, or rocket ships. Satellite Account is a term developed by the United Nations to measure the size of economic sectors that are not included in their own right in national accounts.

A Tourism Satellite Account thus runs alongside national accounts drawing from each sector that has a tourism component without disturbing the totals. It results in figures that measure tourism's true contribution to GDP and allows tourism to be accurately compared to other economic sector listed in national accounts."

TSA also tries to tackle the main challenge of developing such an accounting system. In the words of Mr. Fyfe,"So the challenge for the industry was to develop some standards that would create a virtual industry ...., something that would bring all these sub-components together into one industry that we could show to people and this has been accomplished through this thing called satellite accounts. And now rather than defining the industry only from the consumer or demand side, we have got a balancing piece where we can define it from the supply side as well."[5]

The importance of tourism is often under- estimated as the economic benefits that emerge out of tourism are not adequately estimated. The reason for underestimating the economic benefits that tourism produces is primarily the fact that it is not as visible as other industries such as manufacturing. "In fact tourism activity generates substantial amounts in personal spending, business receipts, employment, income and Government revenue. Only a small part of tourism spending occurs in what are normally considered tourism industry, business such as travel agencies or hotels. A very large part of tourism consumption takes place outside the tourism industries in public and private services such as buses, metro system, museums and also retail shops. But until now there has been no way to measure these economic benefits on an equal footing with other industries such as motor vehicle, oil or tele-communications."[6] Tourism Satellite Account helps in estimating the economic benefits of tourism. "The need for a satellite account for tourism arises because tourism is not an industry in the way industry is defined in the system of national accounts. Instead, tourism is a demand-based concept defined not by its output but by its use. Industries defined in national accounts, such as airlines, hotels and restaurants, etc., produce the same output irrespective of whether it is consumed by tourists or non-tourists. While the total output of these industries is usually captured by the national accounts, it is only the consumption by tourists that defines the tourism economy, e.g., the part of total value added attributable to tourism activities. "Thus, to the extent tourism is an economic phenomenon, it is already embodied in the national accounts but not in a manner readily apparent because commodities and services that are produced and consumed in meeting tourism demand are buried in some other element of the core accounts. The TSA provides a mechanism by which these economic aspects of tourism can be drawn out and analyzed separately but in a way that the results can still be related to the rest of the national accounts."[7]

The ultimate objective of this entire exercise is that it will allow a hard economic case to be made out to facilitate political decision-making for a due place to tourism in the public planning process.

To sum up, Tourism Satellite Account –

- Provides credible data on the economic impact of tourism.

- A standardized framework of putting the data on tourism in a more organised manner.

- It is based on the national accounts data and is not a separate or independent set of accounts.

- Its standard norms are endorsed by the United Nations Statistical Commission and other international organisations so that international comparisons are possible.

- The fundamental structure of TSA relies on a balance existing within the economy between the demand in goods and services and the overall supply of goods and services in the tourism sector.

Tourism Satellite Account is needed because it will increase the knowledge of tourism's importance relative to the overall economic activity of the country and will be a powerful instrument for designing tourism - related policies. It will also create awareness through concrete data about the importance of the tourism activity. It will, among others, enable to measure –

(1) Tourism's contribution to GDP

(2) Tourism's relative position to other economic sectors

(3) Creation of jobs by tourism

(4) Other resources like tax-revenues generated by the tourism industry

(5) Tourism's impact on the balance of payments

(6) The nature and contribution of tourism human resources

(7) The amount of tourism investment and so on.

WTO[8] has summed up the contribution of TSA as follows:-

"Within this context, Tourism Satellite Account will provide:

(a) Macro-economic aggregates to describe the size and the economic importance of tourism, such as Tourism Value Added and Tourism GDP, consistent with similar aggregates for the total economy, and for other productive activities and functional areas of interest; this requires a total consistency with the production boundary of the National Accounts.

(b) Detailed data on tourism consumption, and how this use is met by domestic supply and imports, integrated within tables derived from general supply and use tables of the National Accounts, both at current and constant prices.

(c) Detailed production accounts of the tourism industries including data on employment, linkages with other productive economic activities, and capital formation.

(d) Basic information required for the development of models of economic impact of tourism (at national and supranational level), for the preparation of tourism market-oriented analysis, etc.

(e) A link between economic data and other quantitative information on tourism, such as number of arrivals, forms of tourism, duration of the stay, purpose of the trip, modes of transportation, types of accommodation, existing supply of seat, rooms, beds, rates of occupancy, etc."

No doubt, this is quite an ambitious agenda but happily very effective steps have already been taken to put the agenda in place.

In the 1970s and more specifically in the 1980s many efforts were initiated to develop such a system of accounts. The United Nations, OECD and the WTO were at the forefront of such initiative.

In 1983 in the 5th Session of the General Assembly in New Delhi, the WTO issued a Report showing how the importance of tourism as an economic activity could be established within the national accounting system. In 1991 the international conference in Ottawa accepted Canada's recommended guidelines on Satellite Accounts. As a part of this continuing process, in 1993 the WTO and the United Nations Statistical Commission adopted a common definition of tourism. Australia, Canada, Chile, Dominican Republic, France, Mexico, New Zealand, Norway, Singapore, Sweden, USA, Spain and Italy have already adopted TSA with very definite beneficial results. More than 30 other countries are in various stages of developing the TSA.

The Organisation for Economic Cooperation and Development (OECD) has developed extensive guidelines for the tourism satellite accounts. The OECD's TSA provides recasting of the economic flow data that are already found in the national accounts. It enables the linkage of these data to other important dimensions of tourism such as capital stock estimates, employment and physical features such as the numbers of visitors (both resident and non-resident). It has a comprehensive framework, separate aspects, separate tables, each of analytical use in its own right. Tourism being a demand-based concept, the OECD's TSA provides the mechanism to transform that concept into a means of identifying who produces what for the visitors.

The World Tourism Organisation (WTO) has also developed the Conceptual Framework of Tourism Satellite Account. The emphasis is on analysing tourism activity from both, the 'demand approach' and the 'supply approach'. The 'demand approach' concentrates on 'visitors' and 'tourism consumption'. The 'supply-approach' on the other hand, concentrates on "supply of goods and services specific to tourism". The WTO conceptual framework suggests that the data collected for Tourism Satellite Account should have the following characteristics:-

(a) They should be statistical in character and should be produced on a regular basis.

(b) They should be based on reliable statistical sources.

(c) Data should be comparable over time within the same country, among countries and with other fields of economic activities.

(d) Data should be internally consistent and in tune with the .macro-economic framework internationally recognised.

"The WTO suggests developing the TSA in the form of ten tables. The first three tables identify tourism consumption by products and forms of tourism (inbound, domestic and outbound). The fourth table consolidates total tourism consumption including coverage of tourism consumption in the form of non-monetary transactions to develop estimates of internal tourism consumption. The fifth table presents the production accounts of the tourism industries in a form suitable for comparison with tourism consumption. The next table is essentially the core of the TSA, bringing together the demand and supply sides of the tourism and wherein aggregates like tourism value added and tourism GDP can be evaluated. The WTO recommends countries to focus initially on getting at least these six tables implemented (and also not to emphasize non-monetary flows of tourism consumption in the initial stages of developing a TSA)."[9] Besides, there are tables to assess the employment generated in the tourism industry. The World Travel and Tourism Council presents the Demand and the Supply side of the accounting in the following diagramatic format.[10]

While such efforts have been impressive, the progress on TSA in those countries which need awareness creation on tourism the most, has not been equally impressive. To understand why it has been so, it is necessary to look at the problems that are encountered.

The basic problem, as was pointed out by Mr. Fyfe, was one of perception. The national accounts system in most countries follow a traditional pattern which as in India do not expressly reflect the contribution from the tourism sector. As has been said, how can you measure something that you cannot even identify? The first attempt, therefore, is to have definitional classification that allows such identification and bring all the sub-components into the fold of one industry.

But it is easier said than done. Even if the need for such an identification is accepted, it requires a lot of motivational push to get any action to start the process. Most functionaries under a particular system are allergic to change. The required organisational

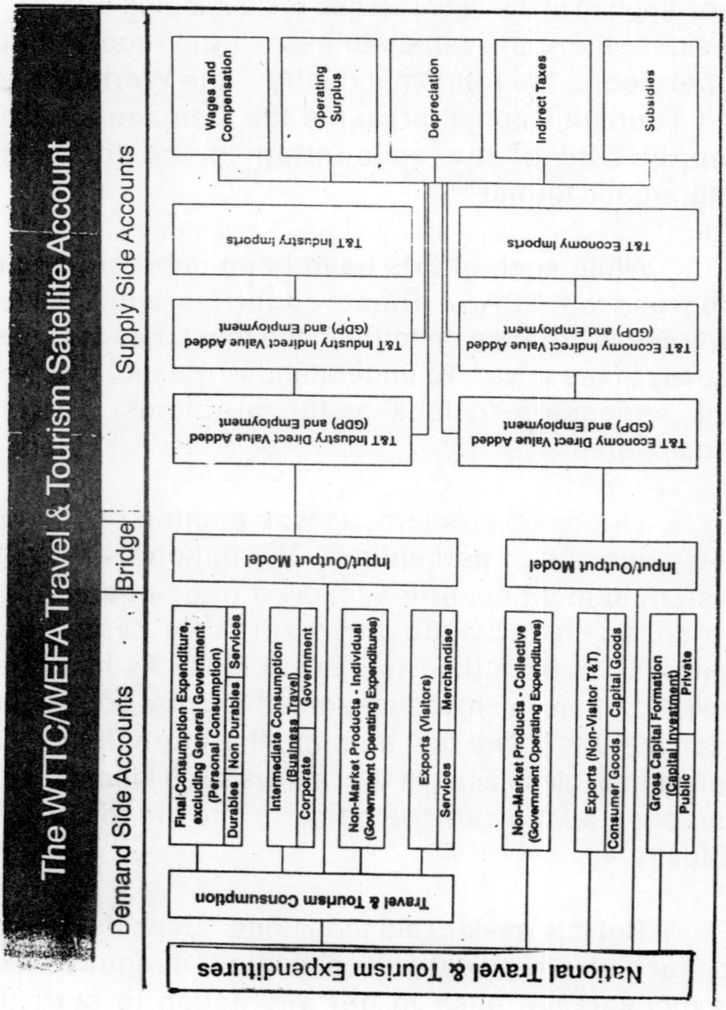
The WTTC/WEFA Travel & Tourism Satellite Account
Demand Side Accounts
Bridge
Supply Side Accounts
National Travel & Tourism Expenditures
Travel & Tourism Consumption
Final Consumption Expenditure, excluding General Government (Personal Consumption)
Durables
Non Durables
Services
Intermediate Consumption (Business Travel)
Corporate
Government
Non-Market Products - Individual (Government Operating Expenditures)
Exports (Visitors)
Services
Merchandise
Non-Market Products - Collective (Government Operating Expenditures)
Exports (Non-Visitor T&T)
Consumer Goods
Capital Goods
Gross Capital Formation (Capital Investment)
Public
Private
Input/Output Model
Input/Output Model
T&T Industry Direct Value Added (GDP) and Employment
T&T Industry Indirect Value Added (GDP) and Employment
T&T Industry Imports
T&T Economy Direct Value Added (GDP) and Employment
T&T Economy Indirect Value Added (GDP) and Employment
T&T Economy Imports
Wages and Compensation
Operating Surplus
Depreciation
Indirect Taxes
Subsidies

system changes will have to be carefully planned and fitted into the State Policy.

While some core definitions have been worked out by the WTO or OECD, it appears that more attention on refinement of the definitions are still needed. What component should go into the tourism industry need to be carefully worked out with flexibility to take into account the specific problems of specific areas. Doug Fyfe again has beautifully illustrated this point with examples from Canada and Mexico. "The crafts industry in Canada is a very small component of the tourism industry because most crafts that are created in Canada are not for the tourists, not even domestic tourists but for the Canadian population at large. So they make some money and they contribute some revenue but a very small part. But in Mexico, which also has a satellite account, the crafts are almost entirely created to sell to tourists, so the value of that economic activity in their satellite account is added in the same way as accommodation at virtually a 100%."[11]

So each country will have to decide on the components that go into the definition of tourism and travel industry. It is precisely because Tourism Satellite Account allows such flexibility that it becomes an acceptable tool for measuring specific impact of tourism.

The adoption of Tourism Satellite Account must start with an attempt to remove a conceptual confusion. TSA uses numbers from national accounts focussing on defined tourism product which are otherwise "invisible". The advantage of TSA is that it is not a new account butis derived from the national account. If the cenceptual confusion could be removed, much of the inhibition and hesitation, perhaps, would be avoided. Any system is allergic to change.Removing the conceptual hurdle, therefore is important to put this change in place. It has to be clearly established that TSA is not a new system of accounts but uses the national accounts to focus on the Tourism sector specifically.

The Indian experience in trying to start the Tourism Satellite Account throws some light on some of the problems faced and which need to be addressed.

One of the immediate fallout of the new policies of liberalisation and globalisation of the economy pursued by the Indian Government since 1992, has been conspicuously felt in the 'service' and other related secondary sectors as a result of increased tourist traffic, both domestic and foreign. The impact has been such that tourism can now claim to be a priority sector that calls for a special attention in the form of such satellite accounting. It is needed not only for an objective evaluation of the investments already made in this sector, but also for a proper evaluation of its increasing importance in the national economy, in earning valuable foreign exchange, in promoting development of remote and inaccessible areas of relatively backward areas through its linkage with the labour - intensive service sectors, etc. In summary, elaboration of a Tourism Satellite Account for India will enable -

- collation and summary of data that is sometimes incoherent or not yet available; and
- measurement of the economic impact of the sector in the national economy.

This account will also answer to a real need for information for all economic agents involved in this sector, including the Government Departments and the private operators. The specific accounting framework is sought to be designed to provide answers to questions such as –

- What economic activities are typical of this sector?
- What economic units are involved in these activities and at what cost?
- What is the level of expenditure in tourism?
- What are the sources of this expenditure?
- Who are the 'beneficiaries' of this expenditure?

The Tourism Satellite Account within the national accounting framework will make for better appreciation of employment in tourism and evaluation of tourism investments and could well give rise to an impact model to facilitate decision making. Knowledge of employment levels in tourism is vital to a better understanding of the possible effects of tourist industry development on employment. Correctly identifying jobs in the sector is the first step after defining the elements that can help create employment.

Over and above the evaluation of tourism investments, strictly speaking investment in related sectors must also be considered: transport, leisure and sports equipment, cultural and scientific assets, the environment, etc. Finally, though it is important to consider the way in which projects are funded by the different economic actors (Government and Public Sector Undertakings, both Central and State, Municipalities, businesses, households), evaluation of the real value of tourism is achieved by integrating elements relating to non-commercial services for tourism. Non-commercial services are those linked to the public service sector that are not already accounted for in contributions such as share holdings for subsidies. Non-commercial services relate to such activities as site development, airport servicing, tourism offices, economic interest groups, etc.

Against this background, in India, an initiative for developing tourism satellite account was taken up. The analysis that follows substantially draws from the Draft Report on Developing TSA in India prepared by the National Council for Applied Economic Research. The preliminary work has been completed by assessing the availability of data in the current statistical system of the country and identified additional data that could be needed to implement a TSA for the Indian economy. The review of the data already available has shown that there are serious data availability concerns that need to be addressed. On demand side, the situation is relatively more encouraging in respect of the data on foreign tourists visiting India as various International Passenger Surveys have been conducted in the past and can be repeated in future. In so far as the domestic tourist statistics is concerned, it has been stated that the available data is not sufficient for being used in TSA. There is no current study which can provide estimates of domestic tourism consumption by households. At the same time, domestic tourism is of such paramount importance in India that any inadequacy of statistics can vitiate the acçounting system. Two problems have been noted –

(i) the total size of domestic tourism expenditure needs to be estimated; and

(ii) the expenditure pattern of domestic tourism needs to be analyzed. This requires primary data collection on domestic expenditure through a comprehensive and broad-based survey.

The Study feels that "The concerns regarding data availability of the supply side are on the whole relatively less strident." A substantial part of some key tourism characteristic industries such as accommodations, meals and transportation, lies in the informal sector. Though enterprise surveys have been conducted by the Ministry of Statistics, Goverment of India for such sectors it is not possible to know how much of the service is utilised by the tourist. Also, for other categories of tourism and tourism-related industries not covered by available surveys, the problems of data availability are more severe. For example, recreation and entertainment expenditure by tourists covers many activities, some of which are included with others (non-tourism related) activities while supply data on others are not available. Many of the developing countries are suffering from lack of data. India has a different problem. India has a tremendous storehouse of statistical information. But, most of the data are related to the basic objectives of planning of the country, namely, poverty alleviation, health, provision of basic needs, etc. Credible numbers for tourism are not collected and are, therefore, not available. Thus while the country has plenty of statistics on very vast areas, sufficient data for formulation of a TSA are not readily available. Moreover, data collection is expensive. Countries may not have resources or the manpower required to develop new data sources and, therefore, they tend to shy away from concepts like the TSA.

Even if we can have the deficiency of primary data collection filled in, then the question will arise as to how can adjust it to the existing national accounts? Besides the issue of non-availability of data, there are other issues which are relevant for development of TSA.

The first is choosing the base year. "The key difference between the TSA and other approaches to measuring tourism in the economy is the integral and seamless link between the formal and the UN system of National Accounts."[12] The reference period in the national accounts is one year that is the same for the TSA. Apart from the problem of the paucity of readily available data and the need to generate new primary data, the study points out that the issue of choosing the benchmark year for implementing the TSA for the economy is an important question to be resolved. For example, the latest available input-output tables for the Indian economy refer to the year 1993-94, some of the auxiliary data sources are from even earlier periods. Yet, at the same time, the primary data to be collected will refer to some future period. Many questions arise. What is the right point in time to fix to build the TSA? Will data collection be a continuous process for each year? Or, a comprehensive survey for a base-year and interpolated later every 5 years. At present there is a mismatch – for example between survey data of arrivals for one year and consumption data of earlier years.

The second issue is of relating to the definition of domestic tourists. In India, the definition of 'domestic tourist' excludes those visiting their native place or hometown. This does not conform to the WTO framework wherein such visits are treated as domestic tourism. Since the magnitude of such travel in India is likely to be quite significant and have a substantial impact on measurement of tourism in the economy, it is worth considering whether the existing definition should be followed or should we instead seek conformity with the WTO definition. If we follow WTO approach is followed, there will be a serious problem in the collection of data.

The third issue is regarding treatment of government travel. The State, it is accepted, occupies a large space in the Indian economy. Therefore, how to treat the nature and extent of Government tourism consumption is a question to be approached. For example, it is asked, should a trip by a Government official in a Government owned vehicle be treated as tourism consumption and his or her accommodation in a Government guest house be viewed the same way as a stay in a hotel? Do such activities really add to tourism in the economy? A related issue is if such an activity is considered as tourism activity and included in the TSA framework, then additional data will be required and it will be necessary to impute value of accommodation in Government owned units when used during Government travel and it will be necessary to evaluate value added to the national economy and hence to the tourism economy. The same considerations would also apply to the travel costs.

The fourth issue pointed out by the study is about the 'same day tourism'. "The international definition of domestic tourism differentiates between day visitors and those tourists who stay away for more than a night but less than 12 months. In both cases the traveller is deemed a tourist if he/she is away from the usual environment. In our system, 'the same day visit' is not included in the tourism statistics. The definition of domestic tourist as used in our country is contingent on the person's stay at hotels or other accommodation establishments for a duration of not less than 24 hours. By definition, it excludes visits to family and more particularly the same day tourism."[13] The relevant question is whether the same day tourism is included within the definition of domestic tourism? It is quite likely that same day tourism must like other types of tourism expands in size and scope as incomes of people increase. The incidence of such activities is more visible now in the metros than it was earlier and is presumably likely to increase in the future.

Tourism statistics are quite important to the countries for framing future policies on developing tourism industry. Tourism activity generates considerable employment and gives a boost to domestic traditional industries. The efforts of World Tourism Organisation (WTO) in defining 'tourism', in introducing the appropriate concepts of tourism statistics and in developing a framework for preparing Tourism Satellite Account (TSA) along with various methods of compilation, is commendable. The WTO, as pointed out, suggests developing the TSA in the form of ten tables. The WTO recommends countries to focus initially on getting at least the first six tables implemented and also not to emphasize non-monetary flows of tourism consumption in the initial stages of developing a TSA. The suggested approach of compiling TSA through the demand and supply sides (thus making it possible to prepare a consistent set of accounts), through the expenditures made by the "Visitor" and the value added of the enterprises comprising the tourism industry, are quite innovative. However, as has been pointed out, the major hurdles are in generating the required data, as the existing statistical systems do not have the sub-classifications to clearly demarcate the tourism sector. The main concerns in developing the TSA would, therefore, be development of tourism statistics. The recent studies also have indicated that development of statistics through expenditure side, may face difficulties in implementation, unless the questionnairs are made considerably eleborate and suitable classifications are introduced. The classifications have been recommended to be elaborate to capture expenditures made by tourists. But, this approach increases the respondent's burden and, therefore, creates further methodological problems in data collection. The alternative suggestion is to build up indicators and use them to move forward the bench-maik estimates of TSA, which can be prepared once in 5 years. It has also been suggested that it may be easier to capture tourism statistics from the supply side, as identification of enterprises catering to the tourism may not be difficult, once industrial classifications (like the International Standar Industrial Classification), are suitably modified to accommodate sub-classifications showing tourism predominant activities. But the moot question will remain – will it serve TSA purpose? In India, therefore, it is as essential to address the problem of collection of tourism statistics as it is to quickly put a TSA in position. At the same time, problems of resource constraints remain and if the most desirable objective of adopting TSA is not to be put in the back-burner, concerted efforts must be made to find ways and means to gather tourism statistics either through the administrative records or minor modifications in the existing statistical surveys on households and enterprises.

Fortunately, many countries have already successfully implemented the TSA and we can draw from their experiences. While attempts are made to put the system in place, it will be useful to give attention to some of the key areas of data collection as we go along. Given below is such a list which is only indicative of action that can be taken up whether or not India decides to introduce TSA, because these requirements can form part of the national accounts system -

i) Development of classification systems (both industrial and product) separately to show tourism related activities.

ii) The enterprises to be classified accordingly (enterprises predominantly engaged in tourism).

iii) Data from these enterprises have to be collected on Item-wise Output, Item-wise Inputs, Salaries and Wages, Operating Surpius/Mixed Income, Number of Employees engaged and Capital Expenditure.

iv) Consumption expenditure statistics of tourists – inbound/outbound/domestic have to be collected from consumption expenditure surveys, as well as budget documents and Annual Accounts of public sector enterprises.

v) Foreign trade statistics have to clearly show tourism goods.

vi) Capital expenditures made by tourism enterprises need to be separately collected.

vii) Tourism statistics have to be collected, according to the consumption approach, production approach and location-wise, notwithstanding the difficulties stated above in collecting tourism statistics according to the consumption approach.

The most important requirement is that the formulation of TSA is to be seen as a national initiative and not just a Ministry of Tourism effort. Since it requires collation of data over a wide range and motivation of the data collecting agencies which are outside the tourism sector, is important, it is essential that awareness about TSA and its importance is spread to policy-makers in the finance and national accounts systems. Only when the impact of tourism becomes visible through cold facts that tourism will gain the rightful priority in the planning process as a catalyst of socio-economic development for the welfare of masses.

References

1. Naisbitt op.cit. p.146
2. World Development Report .. p.
3. Doug Fyfe: Credible Numbers produce Reasonable Decisions. 15th Somnath chib MemMemorial Lecture. Feb. 2000. New Delhi. p.13.
4. WTO: The Economic Impact of Tourism undated pamphlet
5. Doug Fyfe. op.cit. p.14
6. WTO: The Economic Impact of Tourism (pamphlet)
7. NCAER: A Study on Developing a TSA for India. (Draft Report)
8. WTO: Tourism Satellite Account (TSA): The Conceptual Framework. p.3
9. NCAER: A Study on the Development of TSA for India. Draft Report. 2001. New Delhi. p.5
10. WTTC: The WTTC/WEFA Travel and Tourism Satellite Accounting Development Programme. (pamphlet)
11. Fyfe: op.cit. p.15
12. NCAER. Draft Report. p.29.
13. NCAER: op.cit. p.29

3

PILGRIMAGES AND TOURISM*

From time immemorial pilgrimage has been a major component of tourism. India's booming domestic tourism is substantially composed of pilgrim tourist. 'Pilgrim Tourist', therefore, deserves serious attention while planning the overall tourism development schemes.

The interplay between tourism and pilgrimage, however, is not always as simple as it appears to be. It is often said that the link between the two is very old and that the pilgrims were the first tourists. This simple statement, however, raises hoards of difficult issues. First comes the fundamental questions—What is tourism? Who is a tourist? Once, we have answered these questions, we are still confronted with a conceptual problem—should pilgrims be considered to be tourists?

It is well known that the term 'tourism' represents the sum total of a large number of inter-related activities.

---

*Based on the talk "Pilgrimages and Tourism" delivered in India International Centre, New Delhi on 9th May 2000 as part of series on 'Dharma and Development' organized by the Vikram Sarabhai Foundation.

Description of the World Tourism and Travel Council (WTTC) that there are more than 30 activities at the core of what is called 'tourism' has already been discussed. The Constitution of India, under Seventh Schedule (Part XXII), has identified the activities of the Central and State Governments under three 'lists', namely, the 'Central List', the 'State List' and the 'Concurrent List'. Because of such difficulties of definition, perhaps the Constitution of India did not include tourism as such in any one of them.

Quite often, confusion has arisen because 'tourism' and 'travel' are considered the same. There are subtle differences between the two even though both the categories often overlap in our descriptions. For example, Shri Paranjape in his article on "Pilgrim and other travellers"[1] has appropriately described some of the different types of travellers - "Conquerors, prospectors, explorers, traders, scholars, tourists, missionaries, job-seekers, exiles, immigrants, refugees and pilgrims."[1] In this description, the tourist and the pilgrim co-exist as separate identities within a wider generic group of travellers. But, pilgrim tourism or religious tourism comes only as a sub-group of tourism, sometimes even as a sub-group of another group that is generally called cultural or heritage tourism.

Again, forms of tourism also differ depending on the motivation for travel. Based primarily on the apparent motivation for travel, many forms of tourism have emerged — leisure travel or holiday tourism, eco-tourism, cultural tourism, adventure tourism, rural tourism, religious tourism, educational tourism, business tourism, and even political tourism. And, the horizons are ever-expanding. Yet, quite often, the distinction between different forms are not very clear nor are they easily distinguishable. There may be many transitional motivations hidden within the one major objective for travel. The same journey can achieve several objectives.

For the purpose of analysis, however, it is essential to have some basic yardstick and some acceptable definition. The simplest one is the definition given by the World Tourism Organisation (W.T.O.), the apex international organisation for tourism—

> "Tourism—The activities of persons travelling to and staying in places outside their usual environment for not more than one consecutive year for leisure, business and other purposes.
>
> Tourist— (*Overnight visitor*) Visitor staying atleast one night in a collective or private accommodation in the place visited.
>
> Traveller—Any person on a trip between two or more locations."[2]

Though this rather simplistic definition conceals the many difficulties in defining the term. It serves as a good starting point for examining the more fundamental question - are pilgrims tourists? There are different perceptions on this issue and, therefore, the literature on the subject reflects refreshing variety of views. Erik Cohen in his article "Who is a tourist—a conceptual clarification"[3] and "Pilgrimage and Tourism Convergence and Divergence"[4] has referred to the difference between pilgrimage and tourism in terms of the direction of the journey undertaken. The 'pilgrim' is seen as one who travels towards the socio-cultural centre of his or her society while the tourist moves away from it towards the periphery. When the individual's destination is not a pilgrim centre of his religion but belongs to the realm of another religion, culture or society, the individual travelling to it can be classified as a traveller-tourist. However, subsequent studies and experiences have shown that even when the destination is towards a pilgrim centre of his religion, it need not entirely be a pilgrimage. Valene Smith[5] has defined "tourism" as an activity depending on three operative elements—discretionary income" leisure time and social sanctions permissive of travel. 'Pilgrimage' also requires the same three fundamentals. Therefore, to make a distinction based on the direction of travel will be unrealistic. Turner A Turner[6] known for his extensive work on the subject has very appropriately described a tourist as 'half a pilgrim if a pilgrim is half a tourist'.

Individual belief is another salient factor that distinguishes pilgrims from tourists. Tourists are attracted by such belief to places related to religious or spiritual heritage. But, 'tourist—encounters can be just as compelling and almost spiritual in personal meaning'[7]. Smith has referred to the case of an elderly teacher devoting every vacation during her life career to travel and whose final ambition was to see the Great Wall before death. Sheer will-power sustained her journey to this shrine of hers where her tired eyes were suddenly aglow. Once home within a few days to share the delight with her friends and students, she quietly passed on, her wish fulfilled, her pilgrimage done. Thus, while 'faith' is the key element identifying whether a journey is 'tourism' or 'pilgrimage', the term 'faith' itself can have a very wide connotation. Smith has concluded that because of the increased secularization in the West, "distinction between pilgrims and tourists are quite diffuse"[8]. The distinction is blurred in most countries, not necessarily depending on the degree of secularisation. Without going into the philosophical debate about the degree of secularisation in the West or in the East, it is better to accept the fact that the two terms often overlap each other in connotation. Smith describes the situation beautifully, that perhaps, "the pilgrim—tourist path should be considered as two parallel interchangeable lanes, one of which is a secular knowledge based road and the other the sacred road of faith and belief. Then, every guest worldwide could travel either lane or switch between them depending on personal needs or motivations and as appropriate to time, place and cultural circumstances"[9]. This description dilutes the conceptual purity of the term 'pilgrimage' and the true pilgrim may look askance at such a suggestion but nevertheless it is as true a depiction of the reality as one can get.

In the review article "Pilgrims and other Travellers", Paranjape has identified a 'pilgrim' as one who has reverence for the place one is travelling to and is accompanied by vows and absentations and by rituals of self-abasement or humility. A pilgrim of this type even if he comes from a different social background follows all the rituals which are different to his demarcated everyday life. In that sense, explains Paranjpe, there is a role reversal, and the normal order of values changes. The travellers who seek to dominate in the place travelled to, culturally and otherwise also influenced by a similar reverse behaviour. In some context, such role reversal has been called the "away from home syndrome"—the syndrome of a traveller behaving in ways that he would not back home.

In modern times, the motivations for travel, be it for pilgrimage or for tourism, are getting more and more blurred. Smith also refers to 'wish fulfilment' as another powerful and jointly shared motive that provides the impetus to travel. "It is a truism...... that the human species, although endowed with its enlarged brain and association areas, regularly face problems unresolvable by human means.... Hope lies in the appeal to and dispensation from some form of the supernatural...... Pilgrimages are often thought of as journeys undertaken in anticipation of a future betterment, but they need not necessarily be sacred."[10] Examples of such "belief" motivating people to travel are a plenty - the terminally ill seeking a miracle at Lourdes, thousand visiting holy places, or holy-men or miracle-makers in India or elsewhere for succour. Are they pilgrims or half pilgrim-half tourists?

It is not that "hope" of betterment or relief from supernatural powers was a major motivation for travel only in the olden days; even today, with all the scientific advances, it remains a major impetus to travel. The unbelievable scientific developments of the 20th Century have certainly changed our attitude towards life and beliefs. The ever-increasing number of tourists, one would like to believe, are less and less motivated by such beliefs in supernatural powers to travel.

Western scholars, of course, believe that Christianity as a religion had the most direct link to the age of Discovery, Industrial Revolution and the rise of humanism in the post-industrial society. Smith has grouped western thoughts in relation to pilgrimage and tourism into four periods. He states that the Biblical scholars usually mark the Judaic- Christian - Islamic history with the pilgrimage of Abraham, who in obedience to the word of the Lord went to the Promised Land. As early as the 2nd Century, Christian pilgrimages started with visits to places associated with relics. The Crusades renewed this spirit of pilgrimage. Though most writers believe that in those days only the few priviledged and the rich could travel, historical accounts show that in the 11th and 12th Century as many as half a million people visited Santiago. Even, in those heydays of faith motivating travel, one cannot say that undiluted pilgrimage was the sole motivation. Many chronicles talk about like-minded people who go on pilgrimages not out of devotion, but of curiosity and the novelty of the experience.

The next western period of travel from 1517 to 1859 was an exciting period. It was a period of renaissance and reformation, of colonialism, of adventure and discovery, of the great industrial revolution. Whatever may be the motivation—seeking knowledge, immigrating to avoid religion persecution, spirit of adventure, etc.,—travel became much more commonplace and fashionable enough to prompt Thomas Cook in 1841 to become the first tour operator.

In the next hundred years, for the first time in two millennia, traditional belief in God was being seriously questioned (Smith). Apart from opening up of new frontiers of science, Darwin's "the Origin of Species" caused maximum ripples in the stoic socio-political thinking. The introduction of jet flights completely changed the travel and tourism scenario. There was unmistakable boom in tourism, sustained in increasing tempo in the succeeding decades by great scientific and technical advances. The trend was clear—it was the emergence of leisure, pleasure, secular travel in a big way.

Does it imply decline and demise of pilgrimage or pilgrim tourism? There are not enough statistical data but, whatever there is, does not provide any conclusive evidence. Smith again refers to the 1986-87 exit-survey of passengers in Jerusalem which indicated that 55 percent of the 1.52 million surveyed were Christians and 40 percent of them indicated that they had come for a Holy Land pilgrimage. But, Smith again asks the question "Are they true pilgrims on a spiritual journey or were they just religious tourists visiting the Holy Land for the purpose of identity with and knowledge of its historic sites?" It is the same recurring question, the thin line between pilgrimage and travel, that comes up everywhere. This question also introduces another element to the already confused scenario by making another subtle distinction between pilgrims on a 'spiritual journey' and 'religious tourists'.

Unfortunately, rational analysis of the trends becomes difficult in the absence of reliable statistical data. Surveys of the type in Israel, referred to are few and far between. In most cases, "pilgrimage" as a motivation does not have an independent identity in statistical categorisation. It is often grouped under the category "others". Normally, this category is not very big. But, in a recent survey, "others" accounted for more than 50 percent of the tourists visiting Saudi Arabia. One can suspect that most of these would be motivated by pilgrimage.

In India, for international tourist arrivals, there is no separate category for pilgrims. Perhaps, they are covered under "others" or may be under culture and heritage. The recent exit-survey of foreign tourists also does not show such categorisation. In the case of domestic tourists, a large number could be primarily tourist pilgrim. A huge number of domestic tourists recorded in places like Vaishnodevi in the State of Jammu & Kashmir, Sabarimala in the State of Kerala or in Tirupati in the State of Andhra Pradesh show that in India a pilgrimage is still a very strong motivation for travel or a that pilgrim tourists dominate the scene.

Turnbull wrote in 1981 about India that "pilgrimages in all its vitality is at work in India today, where for the masses, tourism is economically unthinkable."[11] Since he wrote this article, things have changed substantially in India. Domestic tourism has grown by leaps and bounds over the last few years and so has outbound tourism. Domestic tourism has increased from 136 million in 1995 to more than 170 million in 1999. The number of Indians going abroad has similarly gone up to about 4 million during this period. The steady growth in G.D.P. over the last few years and the projected good growth in the economy in the coming years, tend to make the Turnbull's statement of 1981, that tourism is economically unthinkable for the masses, irrelevant. In fact, the number of domestic tourists in India could perhaps be the largest in the world. The growth in outbound tourists from India similarly has been remarkable. This growth in domestic tourism does not include very large number of pilgrims who travel only for the purpose of pilgrimages. There are no clear statistics of the number of tourists out of the 170 million who combine pilgrimages along with tourism. But, if one looks at the figure of the domestic tourists in the States, the largest numbers are recorded by the States which have prominent pilgrimage centers. As mentioned earlier, many of them perhaps are 'half pilgrims' and many of the pilgrims perhaps will be 'half tourists'.

Turnbull's observation, however, raises another question. Smith had pointed out, more secularisation of the world leads to lesser number of pure pilgrims. Does the large number of pilgrims in India imply that such secularisation has not permeated the common philosophical outlook of the Indians? Such a question would apparently appear irrelevant in a country like India which has enshrined 'secularism', in its Constitution. There must be other explanations for the still pre-ponderant number of pilgrims in India and a search for such explanations may take us to the realms of sociology and cultural history.

At the same time, a large number of tourists, though not apparently pilgrims, will be pilgrims at heart. This tendency of the modern generation to keep religious beliefs as purely personal, has been described by Smith as "privatisation of religion". "In traditional societies, where few religion options prevail, social sanctions prescribe ritual participation, and most individuals conform rather than risk ridicule, ostracism or worse......... However, in the multicultural or plural societies....... individuals increasingly place their religious view "backstage" in their lives......."[12] (Smith).

Erik Cohen has carried the already blurred distinction between pilgrims and tourists—into a further classification of pilgrim-tourists and traveller-tourists. This classification follows from the basic premise that, all of them are tourists, the labels changing according to the importance of the motivation for travel. For example, Buddhist visitors to Sarnath or Bodh Gaya from the monasteries of India could be 'pilgrim tourists' but the Japanese devotees who visit these places, as also other places like Agra, could be 'traveller tourists'. Cohen has emphasized that this is not merely a classificatory difference. "Rather, the attitudes and demeanour of the two kinds of visitors will be wholly different and so will probably be the meaning and consequences of their respective visits for themselves and their destinations."[13]

The impact of tourism on the pilgrim places has been studied widely and worldwide. The empirical studies have generally referred to the adverse impact of tourism. Cohen's study of the pilgrimage centres in Thailand ends with the observation that with the development of modern tourism, some of the traditional festivals at the popular pilgrimage centres tend to become highly commercialised. In the new forms, the touristic character predominates at the expense of the religious. Tourism promotion is attendant with the apprehension of erosion of cultural and religious values even though there are many instances of positive impact of tourism and of tourism reviving old dying art and craft forms.

In the Himalayan "Shang-rila" of India,—Ladakh, this problem was discussed and debated by Ladakhis and those who are concerned about invasion of tourism into the values of religion and society. There were two major events on this subject in 1995 and 1996. The 'Public Hearing on Environment and Development' organized by the People's Commission on Environment and Development in Leh on 23rd August 1996 and the Seminar on "Tourism Development" on 17th-18th September, 1995 at Leh highlighted the major problems that tourism created for Ladakh and, for that matter, for other such heritage sites. At the same time, the

Seminar, reflected on the positive aspects of tourism in an area not commonly appreciated, i.e., in boosting self-confidence and pride of the local people. Sonam Wangchuk stated in the Public Hearing in Leh - "but there are two totally contradictory effects, one of consolidating and strengthening Ladakhi culture...... The direct interaction with people from developed and industrialized world, who had seen the darker side of modernization and were impressed by the sustainable lifestyles of Ladakh, acted as a most potent educational tool to revive the self-confidence and cultural pride of Ladakhis."[14]

Nevertheless, the concern about the adverse impact of tourism on culture and environment is manifest in many policy documents. The only reference that the Report of the National Committee on Tourism make to pilgrim tourism is in respect of the damage caused to environment by mass pilgrimages. The Report specifically refers to the damage to the environs around the Ganges.

No doubt, all over the world, invasion of pilgrim tourism has changed the character of pilgrim places. The eternal city of Varanasi, is an example. At the same time, there is a tremendous belief that the faith which motivates these millions can also be a binding factor for collective action on sustainable tourism. The 'Interfaith ceremony' held in the Bascillica of St. Francis in 1986 culminated with the Declaration on Nature by the five participating religions—Buddhism, Christianity, Hinduism, Islam and Judaism. For the first time in history, the leaders of these faiths publicly pronounced what was implicit in the teachings, that conservation and harmony with nature was the essence of all faiths, coming down the ages reflected in the sound traditions established by popular beliefs.

Against this background, it will be worthwhile to have a look at the Government of India Policy relating to pilgrimage and tourism. Government's Policy Statements relating to the overall subject of tourism can be found primarily in the Five Year Plan documents. Pilgrimage as a major focus of attention, has not figured in any of the Policy Statements, though there has been cursory reference to pilgrimage as a form of travel and tourism. The other documents in this regard are 1982 National Tourism Policy Statement; 1988 Report of the National Committee on Tourism; 1992 National Action Plan and the 1997 Revised Draft National Tourism Policy".

In the 1982 Policy, there is no specific mention about pilgrimage. There is a passing reference to it under the heading "Domestic Tourism".

> "For the large number of our people who travel on pilgrimage or as tourists, facilities provided are minimal. It will, therefore, be our endeavour to substantially improve and expand facilities for domestic tourists".[15]

The 1988 National Committee, as mentioned earlier, talks only about the adverse impact of pilgrim tourism.

"It is well-known that the pilgrim goes to a place with a sense of reverence and respect, and an ecologically harmonious behaviour is usually built into his or her psyche. However, in an effort to provide 'modern' amenities and to cash in on such mass pilgrimages, Governmental or private agencies have disregarded this factor. The ecological damage being caused in places like Gangotri is typical of the consequences of such short-sighted development".[16]

In 1992 Action Plan, there is a separate section devoted to Pilgrim Tourism, but it only talks about quantitative allocation to improve facilities for tourists for pilgrim centres.

"Pilgrim flows account for a very large percentage of domestic tourism. Infrastructure facilities for tourists for pilgrim centres need to be substantially improved. For this purpose, the Central Government will earmark a sum of Rs. 5.00 crores as Central assistance every year to enable State Tourism Development Corporations/private entrepreneurs to set up or improve accommodation facilities, way-side amenities and transport systems at important pilgrim centres".[17]

The Draft National Tourism Policy of 1997 refers to proper development of pilgrim tourism.

"The main strength of Indian tourism at present is its cultural attractions, particularly, the large number of monuments and archaeological

> remains scattered throughout the country, its art and artefacts and colourful fairs and festivals. The country is also endowed with a number of other tourist attractions and options including beach tourism, forests, wildlife and landscapes for ecotourism, snow, river and mountain peaks for adventure tourism, health resources and farms for health tourism, technological parks and science museums for science tourism, centres of pilgrimage for spritrual tourism, etc. .... The policy, therefore, would be to diversify the tourism product in such a way that it supplements the mainstream of cultural tourism".[18]

In reality, the role of the Government, both at the Centre and in the States, has been confined all these years to providing assistance to create facilities around the pilgrim centres. Most of the places suffer from lack of basic infrastructure and amenities. In most cases, these places are managed by non-official Trusts and other bodies, and in general leave much to be desired in their management. In recent times, considering the tremendous public interest involved, there have been many cases of the Government stepping in, to take up the management of such pilgrim places, combining in such management, the, requirements of both the pilgrim as well as the pilgrim tourists.

The conceptual distinction between 'Pilgrimage' and 'Tourism' is, as we have seen, blurred. In India a very large number of pilgrims are still pure pilgrims motivated to travel purely by faith. Whatever way we call them —

the secular or the sacred, the sheer number of pilgrims are mind-boggling. Many of these, like the Haj pilgrimage, the Amarnath Yatra, the Kumbh Mela require extensive national commitment, and management. Pilgrimage in India—seasonal, regular or otherwise is an important part of tourism, of culture, of heritage and of national activity. Often they create civic problems, put great pressure of the eco-systems and create environmental strain unless properly managed. Pilgrim tourism, therefore, needs to be fitted more closely into the national tourism planning".

A National Policy for management of these centres irrespective of the conceptual problems is, therefore, very necessary.

Reference

1. Paranjape, Makarand :" pilgrim and other travellars." In India International Centre Quarterly. p,10.
2. W. T. O. International Tourism: A Global Perspective Ed. Chuck Y Gee Madrid. 1997 p. 5.
3. Cohen, E "Who is a Tourist? A conceptual clarication" Sociological Review Vol. 22 No. 4 1974.
4. Cohen, E "Pilgrimage And Tourism: Convergence and Divergence" In Journeys to Sacred Places. Ed E.A. Horinis. West port CT. greenwood Press. 1991.
5. Smith Valene. "The Quest in Quest." Annals of Tourism Research. Vol. 19 No. 1 p. 1 1992.
6. Turner V. and E. Turner. Image and Pilgrims in Christian Culture:
7. Smith, Valene. op. cit. p. 2.
8. Smith, Valene. op. cit. p. 15.
9. Smith, Valene. op. cit. p. 15.

10. Smith, Valene. op. cit. p. 6.
11. Turnbull, C. "A Pilgrimage in India" In Natural History Vol. 90 No. 7 p. 16.
12. Smith, Valene. Op.. cit. p.14.
13. Cohen, Erik "Pilgrimage Centre : Concentric and Excentric "India Annals of Tourism Research Vol 19 no. 1 p. 49 1992
14. Wangchuk S. Public Hearing on Environment and Development Leh. August 23, 1996. People's Commission on Environment and Development . India p. 21.
15. Ministry of Tourism, Government of India- Tourism Policy. (presented in both House of Parliament November 3, 1982) para 6.1.
16. Report of the National Commmittee on Tourism : Planning Commission of India, New Delhi, May 1988, p. 123.
17. Govt. of India, Ministry of Civil Aviation and Tourism- National Action Plan for Tourism, May 1992 para 9.
18. Govt. oт India, Ministry of Civil Aviation and Tourism – Draft National Tourism Policy (unpublished) 1997 para 4.7.

4

CULTURE, HERITAGE AND TOURISM

"The forest drips and glows with green
The tree-frog croaks his far-off song.
His voice is stillness, moss and rain
Drunk from the forest ages long.
We cannot understand that call
Unless we move into his dream,
Where all is one and one is all......."

Judith Wright
"Rainforest"

Culture, heritage and tourism always have strong inter-dependent relationship through the ages. Culture and heritage have always provided the major motivation for travel for the largest group of people. Even in present times, the primary motivation for travel continues to be enjoyment of culture and heritage products. The WTO has referred to a recent survey of the European Union which shows that about 20% of the tourists travel solely for experiencing culture and heritage whereas for 60% of visitors, culture is a major source of concern. This figure is only likely to be higher in countries like India which have such rich heritage and tradition.

However, tourism also is a form of leisure and when leisure becomes an industry, culture is also exposed to possible adverse impact. We have seen, tourism has two faces – the positive side and the negative one. Even this possible positive and negative impact on culture has to be seen from two angles. In the narrower sense, we have to look at the impact on the physical-cultural endowments, that is, cultural heritage and products like monuments, etc. In the wider sense, we have to look at the impact on the socio-cultural ethos of a place. Culture of a society is not simply its art, architecture and monuments but extends to the everyday life of the people and the environment around that lifestyle.

Management of sustainable tourism relates to minimising the adverse impact of tourism on the culture of a place in the broad perspective. The people of the host destinations have the primary responsibility for the maintenance and preservation of the culture of the place. At the same time, the tourist also should be sensitised to the host community's culture and the way of life of the people. They should develop respect for the local traditions, beliefs and customs. Only when there is a blend of mutual respect, can the experience be a happy one for the tourists and the host communities alike. To a large extent, the responsibility of the host community also extends to creating awareness among those who come into contact with their culture. The host community has to take visible steps for preserving the best in their culture.

The scope of sustainable tourism is wide-ranging and its nature also would be varied depending on the necessity of a particular situation. However, Naisbitt, whose book we have referred to earlier, has pointed out that such concern should primarily include three major areas:

First is the question of quality. This refers to the quality of experience for the visitors and the need to improve the quality of life of the host community while protecting the quality of the environment.

Second, tourism should be based on the continuity of the natural resources upon which it is based and also on the continuity of the culture of the host community.

Finally, all the stakeholders must ensure that there is a balance between the needs of the tourism industry and the supporters of environmental concerns and the economic needs of the local community. Quite often, it is seen that if such a balance is not achieved and if heritage preservation and environmental concerns are pursued only in isolation, they may result in what is called "counter- development".

We have already touched upon possible adverse impact of tourism on culture. We have referred to the Ladakh experience as an example. This experience throws light on some issues which need attention. Tourism creates in essence a situation of cultural clash in which values of the society change, not necessarily for the worse. Traditions get a jolt. Economic impact also is equally dominant. Tourism suddenly provides unexpected sources of income and in the process, culture becomes a commodity. This is a very common problem posed by market-led economy. Such invasion into the culture can be meaningfully prevented only if the initiative comes from the community itself. Many of the small isolated communities suddenly exposed to. mass tourism also experience social tension and conflict arising out of immigration of workers to manage the tourism demand. Smaller communities which do not have capacities or the manpower to provide the services cannot prevent such immigration which takes place whenever there is a vacuum. Civic amenities come under pressure in such situation causing irritation and environmental degradation, as we have already noted.

Happily, there are plenty of examples of positive impact and we have also referred to some of them quoted by Naisbitt. However, for any rational understanding of the issues, following few points may have to be kept in view –

(1) Tourism is not necessarily the only or the most important agent of change. Liberalisation and globalisation have led to cultural invasion even without contact. Such invasion is in essence much more compulsive and comprehensive. Focussing only on the one area of impact through tourism which in fact could be only minimal, may make us lose sight of the more potential dangers.

(2) Most of the cultural clashes and adverse impact flow from ignorance rather than

insensitivity. Many writers have referred to the "away from home syndrome" – tendency of tourists to behave irrationally away from home.

(3) Quite often, we tend to underplay the strength and resilience of the local cultural values and their capacity to withstand undesirable impact. We had noted, how in a small community like Ladakh cultural contact with outsiders revived self-confidence and pride of the local community.

(4) In a large measure, therefore, the impact of interaction between culture, heritage and tourism will depend on the nature of local cultural and social action. Cultural moorings are also affected by the general process of development. Heritage nurtured with local social care tend to be neglected by the process of urbanisation. Local craft and art which maintain such products become unavailable and the cultural heritage deteriorates. Many of these traditions even become extinct.

Culture develops over a period of time blended with the evolution of the society itself. Any contemplation to make it immune to adverse impact may sometimes lead to clash with the natural evolutionary process itself. Conscious action for preservation of culture and heritage also is bound to be long-term and not *ad hoc*. In the short-term, however, it will depend entirely on how the local community sees the balance between culture and economic gain and how effectively the people are mobilised by social action. Such short-term measures should, therefore, revolve around creating awareness among the people and providing visitors with scientific and easily accessible pre-travel information, on site interpretation, and modern orientation as well as 'virtual reality' experience.

Even if tourism is not always the only or the most important agency for adverse impact on culture and heritage, in any situation like India where heritage is at the core of the tourism product, its preservation even in the physical form should be a major concern. Mr. Alexis Hatzidakis, Architect and Planner in "The impact of tourism on cultural heritage and the environment – preservation and development of traditional settlements in Greece" while making an assessment of the impact of tourism on culture and heritage has made a few observations relating to preservation of heritage. A holistic approach to preservation should revolve around the concept of carrying capacity so that the positive aspects are preserved and the negative ones are minimised. But, carrying capacity consideration may adversely affect the economic aspirations of the local community. Therefore, participation of the local community in the process and creation of awareness is of equal importance. The constraints often faced in such efforts to preserve the physical-cultural heritage can be identified as -

(a) Funding shortage

(b) Controversial social acceptability of the project, that is, contradictions between various groups of interest

(c) Lack of synergy with other State or public policies

(d) Lack of bureaucratic innovation

(e) Contradictions between local and national authorities' priorities or between public and private objectives

Synergy of various sectors is, therefore, a very important part of heritage preservation strategy. In such a situation, national Government can play a very key role. Mr. Hatzidakis has identified the following role for the Government -

(1) creating a platform for the synergy of various sectors;
(2) providing an appropriate legal framework to ensure a sustainable development approach;
(3) encouraging specific activities through financial or other incentives;
(4) promoting training in tourist services; and
(5) providing publicity at national and international level.

Most analysis on the issues of preservation emphasise the importance of Government initiative. The Conference of the Commission on Sustainable Development of the Economic and Social Council of United Nations from 19th-30th April, 1999 also considered that Government could play a significant role in taking forward the Agenda 21. They see the primary role of the Government as one of blending of the initiatives of all the players like the NGOs, local incentives and the private sectors. The Commission highlights the importance of capacity-building work, providing institutional legal, economic, social and environmental framework and taking positive steps for creating awareness. The International Council on Monuments and Sites (ICOMOS) also has placed importance on the following principles in relation to Cultural Tourism Charter:

(a) Since tourism is a strong vehicle for cultural action, the State should provide opportunities for the host community and the visitors to experience and understand heritage and culture.

(b) Since the relationship between heritage and tourism is dynamic, and may involve conflicting values, conscious management in a sustainable way is a responsibility of the Government.

(c) The host community and the local people should be involved in planning for conservation and tourism.

(d) Tourism and conservation activities should benefit the host community.

(e) Tourism promotion programme should protect and enhance natural and cultural heritage characteristics.

It is quite clear that cultural and heritage preservation is not only a question of intention but also requires professional managerial intervention. Tourism is a very fragile sector dependent upon many players, sensitive to the society, environment and the economy. We have analyzed earlier how mass tourism can overwhelm destinations at national or regional level. Dr.Edward W. Manning in his paper "Governance for Tourism – Consulting and Audit Verification Canada" (June 1998) mentioned how Malta in the late 1980s showed that there was less than 28 cm of beach per tourist in the peak season. The chart below given by Dr. Manning shows how in many countries tourists overwhelm the local population.

Management of culture and heritage and tourism sites needs a holistic approach, otherwise even the best of plans may not succeed. As an important economic sector, tourism is often handled individually though its comprehensive linkages with many invisible sectors create serious management problems.

Impact, positive or negative needs constant watch for management plans. It is necessary to watch out for early warning system. Carrying capacity study is a major management tool though, as pointed out by Dr. Manning, there is not one variable that defines carrying capacity completely. On the basis of WTO's formulations, Dr. Manning has charted the few indicators as reproduced below which provide good guidelines for management:

The overwhelming and the overriding lesson that comes out from all this analysis is that tourism cannot be planned in isolation from the planning process of the entire destination. As Dr. Manning points out, destination management and preservation of culture and heritage is a management problem. "The continuing growth of tourism, particularly tourism directed at the most fragile cultures and environments, will test the ability of the industry to manage its impacts and will continue to challenge Government efforts to obtain the desired benefits without the associated problems. Governments need to consider the entire range of tools at their disposal to ensure that "sustainable destinations" are the principal product. Tourism can serve as the engine for sustainable forms of community and regional development but only if the challenge of governance can be met."

The management and preservation of monuments in India by the Archaeological Survey of India could be an illustration of the management problems mentioned above. Talking only of physical heritage, preservation and promotion of heritage in India is distinguished by a very wide variety of heritage, enormity of the problem and difficulties in resource generation both financial and human. The variety of the heritage product covers the large number of national protected monuments and also heritage not protected but fairly old. There are 16 cultural world heritage sites and 5 natural heritage sites. Heritage also includes cities like Varanasi considered to be the oldest living city in the world and places like Hampi which is a excavated heritage town or Khajuraho which has developed around heritage monuments. This heritage also includes heritage buildings which are part of the urban lifestyle of the people. They also reflect vividly the development of a place and symbolise the growth of civilization and the culture of a particular place. Cities like Kolkata, Mumbai, Old Delhi, etc., are living monuments of the evolving civilization of the place. Within these different groups again, there is a great variety and wide-ranging time span. For instance, some of the heritage like Ajanta caves can be traced to the period before the Christ. There are places like Sanchi, Ellora, etc., ranging between Fifth to Thirteenth Century A.D., the wonderful Taj Mahal of the Seventeenth Century, Ashokan rock-edicts of the period before Christ and thousands of heritage which are between 100 to 300 years old. This variety of Indian heritage must also refer to the pilgrim destinations which have carried on traditions from time immemorial. The special features of Indian cultural heritage also refer to –

(1) The living heritage, for example, of people who continue to live in the monastic settlements located high in the Himalayas.
(2) Exquisitely carved temple towns of the South.
(3) Desert fortification of the West.

The enormity of the problem can be gauged from the fact that there are about 5,500 monuments declared as 'protected monuments' by the Archaeological Survey of India. There are more than 5,000 such monuments looked after by the State Governments and there may be thousand others which are not looked after by anyone. There are large number of heritage products which are more than 1000 years old and a large number are between 500 and 700 years old.

The efforts for preservation of heritage in India can be grouped under three aspects: regulatory, preventive and collaborative.

So far as regulatory aspect is concerned, there is a very well established system and machineries going back to 150 years. As far back as 1861, the Archaeological Survey of India was set up for central regulation of heritage monuments. In 1904 the "Ancient Monuments Preservation Act for Protection and Preservation" was passed. In 1958, a comprehensive legislation called "Ancient Monuments and Architectural Sites and Remains Act, 1958" was passed. The Conservation Manual of 1923 lays down the basic approach to preservation, that is, authenticity.

There are four broad aspects of the management of preservation and regulation.

First, the physical dimension which relates to identifying the structure of designs, use of materials to suit the particular climate or particular specificity of a place.

Second, Structural engineering and technical details of maintenance which includes restoration technology.

Third, the artistic part that is, taking care of art work, paintings, carvings, etc.

Fourth, the most important responsibility of designing the carrying capacity and imparting authenticity to the act of maintenance and preservation.

The preventive aspect of maintenance is also equally important. The 1958 Act provides for punishment for those who destroy, remove, injure, alter or deface a protected monument. It also lays down that no construction or mining is allowed in a radius of 100 meters which is declared as a prohibited area. Area upto after 200 meters is considered a regulated area where any activity can be taken up only with a 'no objection certificate' from the Archaeological Survey of India.

The maintenance and regulation of heritage is a big responsibility which requires collaboration with many other players. It requires –

(a) Coordination with other Ministries like Tourism and Urban Development.

(b) Combined programme of creating awareness about the importance of this heritage.

(c) Making people participate in its preservation by inculcating a sense of pride among the local people.

(d) Involvement of youth in the awareness programme.

The budget available for maintenance of such huge number of monuments is totally inadequate. In order to overcome the resource problems, the Government of India have created a National Culture Fund. It is a trust created in 1966 with professional management drawn from corporate sector, private foundations and non-profit voluntary organisations to promote and preserve culture. Financial contributions and donations are 100% tax deductable and foreign donations can be received under the Foreign Contribution Regulation Act. The fund can also facilitate donor specific project pertaining to heritage monuments. Happily, various non-governmental organisations like the Indian National Trust for Arts and Cultural Heritage (INTACH) have taken up restoration and preservation work around the country. Multinational Corporations like the American Express have also funded such activities of restoration. In a recent move, the Department of Culture have allowed private sector to maintain the surroundings of national monuments and to provide public facilities.

Yet the task is heavy. Most heritage have shown signs of decay. Proper ambience is missing in even the protected monuments. Public vandalism and graffiti, etc., have damaged invaluable heritage.

5

India–Untapped Potential

In Chapter-I, we had analysed India's present tourism achievements and had seen how inadequate it is compared to other neighbouring countries and compared to India's own potentials. We can also re-count WTTC's assesment of the future potentials.

The World Tourism and Travel Council (WTTC) has estimated that India's travel and tourism potentials can provide, in another 10 years time (by 2010) its economy substantial resources - Rs. 500,000 crores in contribution to GDP, Rs. 130,000 crores in capital investment and Rs. 160,000 crores in export earnings. It could also create, during this period, in the tourism and travel economy, 7 million new jobs. If properly harnessed. the WTTC feels, travel and tourism can account for one job out of every 15 created in India.

Even at present, it is well known, tourism provides the second highest net foreign exchange earnings to the economy at Rs.12,000 crores or about $3 billion. Yet, the WTTC's projections of potential growth and contributions of tourism appear quite staggering in the present scenario. Today, tourism's share in the GDP is 1.2 percent and of employment 2.4

per cent. The WTTC estimates show that these shares can go, up to 7 percent and 3.5 percent respectively in 10 years time with some extra national initiative.

The statistical projections, however, have their own inherent problems. First, there is no accepted definition of tourism as such. Tourism comprises of so many activities - many of them are invisible that a common denominator is difficult to find. The WTTC has identified more than 30 activities to be at the core of the tourism business. WTTC defins 'travel and tourism industry' which includes activities traditionally associated with travel and tourism such as catering. transport and accommodation. This differs from 'travel and tourism economy' which takes into account the impact of travel and tourism and its 'flow through' effect across the wider economy. Moreover, many of the activities in the tourism sector cannot be easily quantified and, therefore, the economic impact tends to be under-measured. International comparisons are also constrained by astounding difference in the matter of data collection and interpretation.

Such difficulties in measurement notwithstanding, it is a widely shared general perception that India's achievements in tourism have not been in keping with the potentials. It is difficult to adequately describe the potentials but the oft-quoted expression that India offers 'the world in one place' and that India has got 'everything for everyone for all seasons,' briefly sums up the essence. In more concrete terms, people talk about the potentials in relation to the wide variety of physical, geographical attractions and natural beauty, rich cultural heritage flowing from an ancient civilisation, colorful and vibrant population, each area and each community in the vast country being unique in its lifestyle and culture.

The potentials of tourism in India can be better appreciated and viewed against the global scenario. Globally tourism arrivals have reached 635 million and receipts excluding receipts from international transport etc., have touched $439 billion. Tourism employment is 10.6 percent of the global workforce and tourism contributes 10.2 percent towards GDP, generates tax revenues of $655 billion and its gross output is $3.4 trillion. Therefore, while the projections about India's potential made by the WTTC may appear very ambitious seen in isolation, in the global context they appear quite achievable.

However, an assessment of the progress made so far and of the present achievements will leave a large number of nagging questions unanswered. India receives only about 0.4 percent of the total international tourist arrivals and is placed 44th among the nations. The share of tourism in the GDP is around 1.2 percent. It is not that India has not made progress over the years. From beginning of 17,000 international arrivals in 1950 contributing Rs.7.7 crores to the economy, present arrival of 2.64 million tourists contributing about $3.5 billion in foreign exchange earnings is certainly a substantial progress. In addition, the number of domestic tourists has swelled to a massive 176 million.

In the early stages of tourism planning, the focus was on domestic tourism. Tourism was seen as a bridge between people, an instrument for creating friendship and harmony, and an avenue for giving shape to the spirit of adventure among the youth of the country. The 1982 Tourism Policy of India, the only Policy Statement so far, states the objectives to be to so develop tourism that -

"(i) It becomes a unifying force nationally and internationally fostering better understanding through travel.

(ii) It helps to preserve, retain and enrich our world-view and life-style.

(iii) It brings socio-economic benefits to the community and the State.

(iv) It gives a direction and opportunity to the youth of the country.

(v) It also offers opportunities to the youth of the country not only for employment but also for taking up activities of nation building."

India's progress in tourism is, therefore, marked by a paradox. The progress made in achieving the policy objective of encouraging domestic tourism has been generally satisfactory, however inadequate the infrastructure may be and however unsatisfactory the services are. But, growth in international tourism has been way behind other nations, including our neighbouring countries in South-East Asia.

It is true that such comparison is logically flawed. It is not correct to compare only one segment without referring to the whole. Tourism is a totality of many activities. Therefore, a country's total economic policy will also influence the pace of tourism growth. But, a more comparable picture perhaps could be of Mexico - a country in economic doldrums in the 80's. Today, in terms of international arrivals, it is 7th in the world, earning $ 7.9 billion. Tourism was an engine of growth for the Mexican economy.

Tourism in India has not yet received that focus of a national activity. The potential of tourism as an input in the growth process is not reflected in the economic policy documents. Tourism development in India is also afflicted by the fact that awareness and sensitivity about the potentials of tourism has not percolated to all sections of the society.

The lack of sensitivity also has affected the ambience of most of the tourist attractions and has put tremendous pressure on the country's priceless heritage. About 5,500 heritage monuments protected by the Archaeological Survey of India and another 5,000 or so looked after by the State Archaeological Departments suffer seriously from lack of resources for maintenance.

Another drawback of the Indian situation is the absence of participation by the people both in promoting and in benefiting from the realisation of the tourism potentials.

There is too much of dependence on the Government. Basically, most of the tourism activities should be private sector driven and the Government should play the role of a regulator for ensuring sustainable development and facilitator for encouraging private initiative. Over the years, a number of incentives have been developed to encourage private initiative, but most of them appear to have been the results of *ad hoc* reaction to demands from the industry rather than being part of a comprehensive long-term plan. On the other hand, the tourism sector has often complained of multiplicity of taxes and high level of taxation. Some of the international comparisons have shown Indian tourism sector to one of the highest taxed. Even the inter-State tourist transporters are clamouring for rationalisation of taxes imposed by various State Governments.

It is well known that lack of adequate infrastructure is the primary constraint in achieving the full potentials. India is a longhaul destination for most tourists because the generating markets that India primarily depend on are far away. Therefore, to attract more people to come to India, the overall welcome and the incentives will have to be better than those offered by competing destinations.

"A number of small things which add up to making a place an attractive destination will have to be looked into. Most important is the issue of making access to India easy. The visa formalities should be simplified and computerised for easy verification. Tourists, who have so many competing options, will be attracted to places to which communication is easy and inexpensive.

Most of the countries which have made rapid progress in tourism in recent times are distinguished by easy availability of air-seat capacity, modern and efficient air transport handling facilities and free access by charter flights. These are areas which need urgent attention in India. The *de facto* capacity now available may be less than the desirable level in view of the increasing number of Indians travelling abroad and ease of access to our competing neighbouring countries in South-East Asia. Similarly, internal connectivity to important places of tourist attraction has not always been optimal. Khajuraho languished for years because of this deficiency, so did Ladakh.

In the federal structure of India, promotion of tourism and provision of basic facilities lie primarily with the State Governments. The response of the States to the emerging challenges vary widely. But in totality, the resource allocations by most States for the development of tourism sector have been meagre.

Though such allocations have been increasing in recent years, the total resources available would be limited to around Rs.300 crore. The yearly allocations in the Central budget have long remained around Rs.100 crore only. The situation has improved now. Some States like Andhra Pradesh, Uttar Pradesh, Kerala and Rajasthan substantially increasing their allocations.

But, the Action Plan of the Government in 1993 had set the goal of achieving about 5 million international tourist arrivals by 2000. Another exercise by the Government in 1996 had estimated the financial requirement to achieve this objective at Rs.48,000 crores, of which Rs. 5,300 crores was the investment required in tourism sector in the Central and State Governments over a period of time.

With the range of Government resources available as shown above, and with no significant private enterprise in sight, it is only but natural that the present efforts touch only the fringe of the problems.

If India has to achieve the potentials estimated by WTTC, the future strategy will have to be in tune with the fast changing developments in the travel and tourism sector. The key developments that are expected to shape the future are -

(i) Socio-demographic factors
(ii) Technological revolution
(iii) Changes in consumer behaviour
(iv) Concern for issues of sustainable development
(v) Development of human resource

Slowly the industrialised countries are experiencing declining population growth rates. Economic growth has made it possible for larger number from the developing countries to have leisure and means to travel. China, for example, is expected to generate 100 million outbound tourists by 2020.

The number of two-income households is growing in all countries. These families have more income, desire and time to travel but have less leisure time. Therefore, there will be an increasing number of shorter vacations. Long-haul destinations like India will have to devise new strategies to overcome disadvantages of distance to attract such categories.

The most profound changes, however, will be in relation to technological developments. The Civil Aviation sector, as has been pointed out, would be particularly affected by such changes.

In the next five or six years, the industry is expected to progress to a stage where more than half of the international scheduled journeys will be undertaken with new electronic tickets. Such tremendous changes in the volume of air traffic, in the aircraft design and aviation control techniques, will naturally make the air corridors congested.

These developments will pose many challenges to the national Governments - getting suitable aircraft, upgrading technology and safety norms, meeting the sheer pressure of numbers, and not the least, change of ideology to meet the new challenges.

The pressure of huge number of tourists will also raise issues of preservation and tourism promotion, of carrying and absorbing capacity. Undoubtedly each country will be under closer scrutiny of the media and public organizations on issues like sustainability, drugs and diseases, sex abuses and human rights violation.

How should India, already below its true potentials, prepare to meet these emerging challenges? The WTTC has suggested a four-fold plan of action to move towards achieving the potentials, namely,

(1) make travel and tourism a strategic, economic and employment priority;

(2) move towards open and competitive markets including Civil Aviation liberalisation;

(3) pursue sustainable development; and

(4) eliminate barriers to growth - provide incentives to the private sector and invest in human resources.

Many of these issues are accepted as part of policies of the Government and many policy initiatives have been started on most of these areas. The draft National Tourism Policy centres around creating awareness, people's participation, public-private partnership, strengthening of organisation, creating sustainable tourism, etc., as the key objectives.

Tourism touches everyone's life. Therefore, the list of things to do may be never-ending. But, the most important thing is to make a beginning.

6
TOURISM AND PEACE

"TRAVEL IS THE LANGUAGE OF PEACE"-
MAHATMA GANDHI

We all know that from the dawn of history, tourists and travellers in different forms have been spreading the message of peace and brotherhood. In fact, the pilgrims perhaps are the earliest travellers. The pilgrims, no doubt, were driven by their respective faiths but, in the ultimate, all faiths merged in one common quest for peace with the sublime. As has often been said, that search for peace makes the pilgrim half a tourist, as the tourist becomes half a pilgrim. Search for peace is a pilgrimage in the human history dotted with wars. In India, we proudly refer to the Great Emperor Ashoka, who in the height of his biggest victory saw the futility of it all and embraced Buddhism and the path of non-violence. He sent his children as pilgrims to spread the message of peace and love. Many centuries of search has brought us today to the beginning of another millennium with renewed hopes.

Naturally things have changed—our lives and attitudes have changed. Technological revolution in all spheres of human activities has made possible the ideas which were in the realm of scientific fiction a few years back. The information technology revolution has changed the frontiers of human imagination. George Orwell's "Nineteen Eighty Four" and Aldous Huxley's

"Brave New World" which fired the imagination of earlier generations already look ancient in the light of these developments.

But, this is also a period of renewed hope because the language of peace is more vocal today than ever before. Borders are disappearing, as has been pointed out, "not only for trade capital and information but also for ideas, norms, cultures and values". But, it is tourism which has really made the world a global village, by spreading the common bond of understanding. The fascinating story of tourism's growth from mere 25 million arrivals in 1950 to 698 million in 2000 is well-known. Well-known also is its vast future potentials. Today, only about 7 percent of the potential and capable travellers are actually travelling. With the still unrealised expanse of possibilities, it is not only the biggest industry of the world, but also the biggest single catalyst for peace capable of carrying the message of love, brotherhood and understanding across borders.

Tourism and peace have a symbiotic relationship. Tourism and development can happen only in a climate of peace. On the other hand, it is often said that soldiers rarely violate the frontiers opened up by the warmth of the people. Today, there is increasing acceptance that travel and tourism is one of the most potent weapons for integration and understanding, redistribution of income and for a just and equitable sharing of wealth. But, one has to be pragmatic. Peace has to be pursued on many fronts. Tourism is only one of the means not the only one. One great responsibility of national governments make tourism happen, give it priority attention, facilitate, create partnership, provide infrastructure.

One of the world's earliest economists, Xenophon showed how Athens flourished during peace as did most other States (as quoted by Galbraith in "A history of Economics : The past as the present)." It is so much of an axiomatic truth that it needs no elaboration or illustration. There are, however, numerous examples around the world of the local community striving for an atmosphere of peace in an otherwise disturbed area so that tourism could provide them with income and employment. There are examples in India where in areas predominantly dependent on tourism, public action for peace has been the strongest, often cutting across differences of political and religious faiths.

It is the other aspect of travel and tourisms-its positive impact-that is not often as widely acknowledged. However, that is the philosophy on which the Indian Tourism tradition—'the guest is God'—is based. The Statute of the World Tourism Organisation (WTO) recognises this relationship and, therefore, emphasises not only tourism's contribution to economic development but also to international understanding and peace. And the Manila Declaration on World Tourism says "Its very existence and development depends entirely on the maintenance of a state of lasting peace to which tourism itself is required to contribute". The Pacific Asia Travel Association (PATA), while looking at the future, talks not so much of individual member's marketing interest but of a vision of using tourism to make this world a better place to be" through tourism. So strong was the perceived impact of tourism on integration and understanding that the National Tourism Policy of India put one of the objectives of tourism development as-

'a unifying force nationally and internationally fostering better understanding through travel.'

Today, internally 176 million domestic tourists in addition to more than 100 million pilgrim travellers across India annually have enabled to make the immense diversity of the country a strong focal point for unity.

The Constitution of the UNESCO in 1945 significantly stated that "since wars begin in the minds of men, it is in the minds of men, that the defence of peace must be constructed." The mind has to be liberated to reach to humanity across the borders around which war and peace have always centred in history. The continuing philosophy of the Indian tourism tradition - "The world is one family" eloquently symbolizes this quest. In 1915, the Russian artist Kasmir Malevich (1878-1935) "presented the unrepresentable sublime" by painting a white square on a white background. In his Manifesto of Suprematism, Malevich said: 'I have beaten the lining of the coloured sky, torn it away and in the sack which formed itself, I have put colours and knotted it. Swim! The free white sea, infinity, lies before you'[1].

Tourism has helped to erase the barriers of borders from the minds of men, to provide the human touch to the strongest force of the 21st Century—the process of globalisation.

But, globalisation, everyone realises, is not an unmixed blessing. As the Human Development Report, 1999 points out "the collapse of space, time and borders may be creating a global village........ but billions of others find borders as high as ever". Unless the opportunities and the benefits of globalisation are shared widely and equitably by all mankind, and as long as economic disparities afflict international growth, peace will always be at risk. Tourism, we all agree, is the most pleasant means to ensure transfer of resources without friction. It offers golden economic opportunities for development for those who need them most and, therefore, for bridging the gap between nations. The Human Development Report, 1999 brings our attention to the disconcerting realisation that 60 countries have been getting steadily poorer since 1980. The gap between the richest and the poorest was about 3 to 1 in 1820, 11 to 1 in 1913, 35 to 1 in 1950, 44 to 1 in 1973 and 72 to 1 in 1992. Re-distribution, therefore, is a major concern of the world if peace has to be viable. So said the Pearson Commission 30 years ago as did Nobel Laureate Prof. Tinbergen in recent time. We have realised now that tourism can help in this process of equitable redistribution, therefore, participating in peace.

One can look against this background at the experience of the Caribbean countries. Reportedly, for 30 States in the region, tourism today accounts for 50 to 70 percent of the States' economy. We have to harness this power of tourism for countries with limited opportunities for economic growth.

But, what can happen does not necessarily always happen. More than half the international travellers of today are from high income countries and more than half are travelling to high income countries. The same ratio, therefore, reflects tourism earnings as well. Most of the countries which need the healing touch of re-distribution through tourism are unable to do so because the vicious cycle of their own economic infirmities deprive them of the infrastructural and promotional strength that make tourism possible. We have the risk of losing the most potent tool of promotion of peace unless we take positive action to strengthen the capabilities of those who need tourism most. WTO, WTTC, PATA and all others have to go off the beaten track to provide a weighted support to these countries to enable them to catch up with others in the race in which evolution of economic history placed them behind. The World Bank, the UNDP and other funding institutions must bring tourism from the periphery to the core of their concern.

Peace through tourism can be a reality only if we are alive to many other aspects of globalisation and the unbelievable and ever-accelerating speed of development of technology. Along with free movement of goods and services and world-wide spread of knowledge, globalisation and mass tourism also have to contend with trafficking in drugs, human beings, arms, spread of HIV, not to speak of terrorism and fundamentalism. All the positive possibilities we talk about will lay crumpled in ruined hopes if the travel and tourism industry and all of us who strive to make it a vehicle of peace, fail to act in unison, determination and pragmatism.

Developed countries today dominate the outbound tourism market. All effects of globalisation can be partially countered if the originating countries take steps to sensitise the tourists on these issues. Strict measures against sex-tourism, child prostitution are as much required in the originating countries as in the countries where they are in practice. For millions in the shadows of poverty and starvation these issues may be overwhelmed by the logic of existence. Those who do not have the compulsion of economics as an argument have a lesser logic not to act and greater responsibility to contribute positively to matters that make peace a possibility in the minds of men. The travel and tourism industry also has a key role to play here.

In most countries, tourism revolves around culture and heritage. Culture in all its diversity is the strongest common binding factor for peace. Cultural heritage and tourism bring people together in common sharing and build bridges of peace through mutual understanding. United Nations General Assembly's Proclamation of the Year 2000 as the International Year for Culture of Peace has brought together all over the world organisations and individuals working for peace and understanding. In india, Cultural Resources Conservation Initiative's (CRCI) work in The State of Punjab for restoration of sacred sites as a social process has cut across religious boundaries and has shown that tourism and culture can mobilise people to create an atmosphere for peace. This culture of peace initiative should not remain confined only to a sectoral, one year effort but should be made part of mankind's resolve to thrive for peace continuously.

In India, peace is seen in a wider context of harmony of the human existence with nature. There are also many examples around the world of tourism helping to maintain that harmony. There are many other examples of insensitive exploitation of nature for present economic gains. Unfortunately, the negative ones get more publicity than the positive ones.

The lessons to be learnt are quite clear —

- That harmony of peace, development and environment can be achieved.

- That there are people who believe in this capacity to achieve and their voices need to be heard.

- That conflict between the present economic needs and the needs of future environment can be resolved to the advantage of the present generation.

- Therefore efforts are to be made to

- Make those achievements widely known so that in other areas, courage of conviction can enthuse others who are on the fringe of doubt.

- Start a movement interlinking the efforts of those who are guided by their belief in peace and environment. The movement should start with the people at its core of strategy - creating awareness and making them participate in a movement that gives them economic strength.

Just as global tourism and cultural action can strengthen the global foundation for peace, mass tourism can as well lead to cultural conflict. Positive action at national and international level to protect the cultural diversity should be an integral part of movement for cultural action for peace and cultural exchange.

But, peace is never a passive static dream. In a dynamic reality, peace needs to be pursued and pursuing peace has always been more difficult than pursuing war. The silent majority in the world who always thrive for peace often remain hidden in silence. As Paulo Friere said in a different context, the fundamental theme of the tourist community today, with such strong capacity for action for peace should be "the conquest of its right to a voice, of the right to pronounce its word". How to make the millions of individuals aware of their collective hidden positive power for peace should be the major concern of all organisations.

One way to start it would be to create a movement for awareness. Individually, no tourist may be aware of the strength of his contribution to the collective power. The internal faith of each tourist in peace, his desire to understand the realities and share the human feelings of the places he visits, has to be given a language. Each one has to be made aware of his being part of a conscious movement. Can every ticket he holds, also contain his vow to uphold these ideals and to contribute to it? Such an initiative will make him conscious and quite often, a proud participant in a process, which in any case inwardly perhaps he believes in.

Awareness must involve local people. People will guard peace for tourism if they see benefits of tourism. Often, it is not realised and, therefore, awareness does not come. Measurement of benefits should be apart of the awareness campaign. Such positive action to translate the inherent power of the large human movement that tourism is, would require organizational efforts. There are many - already working with this objective - The WT0 Code of Ethics (Appendix - III) the UNESCO Culture of Peace, The Green Globe, The PATA initiative and so on. Coordination and networking of these initiatives will give shape to the ideas, and strength to the organizations. The objective being the same, it is only logical that shared platform and action will give it more focus.

War, we repeat, begins in the minds of men. Peace also has to generate in the mind, and, therefore, early. 'The child is the father of man'. In the traditional society, the process of liberating the mind would have started at home, in the family. In the nuclear family of today guided by electronic media and technological revolution that advantage is not always available. The shaping of the mind has, therefore, to start primarily in the school. The travel and tourism industry as also the electronic media which feed this industry, has to take on this role of addressing the young minds positively.

The international community needs to work with a sense of urgency.

Reference

1. Sauvik Chakravarti: "Antidote: Essays against the Socialist Indian State.

7

POSTSCRIPT : TRAVEL AND TOURISM AFTER 11TH SEPTEMBER, 2001

The events of 11th September, 2001 and subsequent geo-political situation, have cast a dark shadow on the Travel and Tourism industry.

As Mr. Kofi Annan, Secretary General of the United Nations pointed out – it is a time to reaffirm faith in values of "peace, freedom, tolerance, human rights, and the very idea of a united human family".

The events affected, said Mr. Annan, "the freedom of human beings to travel, to exchange goods and services – everything a World Trade Center stands for".

The immediate impact of the events on travel and trade has been very severe but the future assessment still remains uncertain. Almost all the premier public and private organisations of travel and tourism have tried to make an assessment and they all agree on a few salient features. First, the psychological impact of the incidents has been far-reaching, changing the perception about safety and security of air travel. Side by side, there are optimistic examples of the resolve of the international community to fight the impact with determination. Second, the future impact will depend on how the international security situation takes shape - whether the operations remain localised or spread to other areas or escalate to a major conflict. Third, the status of the travel and tourism sector will depend, to a large extent, on the trend in the global economy which was passing through a recession before September 11 and was believed to have almost come to the end of that recession. Fourth, most of the assessment, cautious in their optimism are at pains to emphasize that the future is dependent on a wide mix of many unpredictable factors.

The WTO quotes Mr. Horst Cohler, Managing Director of the IMF who made an announcement on 12th September, "Our present statement is that, despite the scale of the human tragedy, these terrible events will have only a limited impact on the international economy and global financial system". The main Central Banks have provided resources to maintain the liquidity of the finance system. The United States Federal Reserve and the European Central Bank have cut their interest rates by half a point. Added to that, exchange rates have not undergone any major changes as regards the previous situation.

• The immediate effect in USA as expected was of panic and caution. The travel and tourism industry was the worst hit. The Travel Business Round Table, a private consultancy assessment report, presented a grim picture of the effects on the US travel and tourism industry[1].

"- Analysts project tourism in the U.S. could drop by nearly one-third in the coming months.

- U.S. airlines are flying with 40 percent to 50 percent of their seats empty, even after drastically reducing their scheduled flights.

- Across the U.S., 25% of conventions and meetings scheduled before the end of 2001 have been cancelled.

- Per-room revenue is projected to decline between 3.5 percent and 5 percent this year the largest decrease in room revenue in 33 years.

- Hotels could lose $2 billion in room revenues and other associated income. Specially, cities around the country are already experiencing tremendous losses.

- Travel agencies are losing an estimated $51 million per day in sales.

- Corporate travel is projected to fall by 50 percent by January 2002.

- One estimate states our economy will decrease by 1.8 percent of total GDP, directly resulting in a loss of 1.1 million U.S. jobs".

The World Travel and Tourism Council feels that despite this immediate adverse impact, the industry will bounce back to its pre-September 11 growth path. However, they have also painted a very grim picture of immediate effects. Based on a standardlised hypothetical case scenario of 10 % decrease in travel and tourism demand, the WTTC has reported the following possible impact on national, regional and world employment and GDP:-

- United Kingdom: Decrease of 1.9% of total GDP for the UK economy and the loss of 190,000 jobs.

- European Union: Decrease of 1.9 % of total GDP for the EU economy and the loss of 1.2 million jobs.

- United States: Decrease of 1.8 % of total GDP for the US economy and the loss of 1.1 million jobs.

- World: Decrease of 1.7 % of total GDP for the world economy and the loss of 8.8 million jobs.

The Stratfor Report prepared for PATA (Pacific Asia Travel Association) referred to the Wall Street Journal which estimated the total cost of the September 11 events at atleast $ 100 billion. The World Bank also estimates that the events of September 11 and developments thereafter will trim one percent of global growth in industrialised countries and 1.3 percent in the developing economies for 2001. There are strong feelings that U.S. vulnerability being so rudely exposed, safety of air travel will not be the same ever again atleast for some time to come. Much will, therefore, depend on the effectiveness of international initiative on curbing terrorism and also on how the geo-political situations unfold.

However, there is strong optimism in many quarters nevertheless on the possible scenario. There is consensus among all analysts that this immediate impact will not be a long-lasting one. The HVS International Journal for October reported that markets which had reported 60-70 percent decrease in occupancy have shown recovery and after heavy cancellations for September and October, bookings in November and December were holding strong and many cancelled trips have been re-booked. The more important question at this time, feels HVS, is the one of tackling recession. Even before September 11, all indicators were pointing towards an economic recovery by March 2002 which most experts now agree will be underway by the end of the year. The HBS projections for the travel and tourism industry reflect the general feeling of most other analysts – that in the short – term the industry will suffer setback but will recover be mid-2002 and in the long – run the industry will bounce back to a growth path stronger than it was before September 11.

In a sense international terrorism and geo – political upheavals had affected tourism earlier also though may not be in the same scale or pattern. One can refer to the terrorist attack on Luxor, the political situation in Fiji or problem in Sri Lanka. The major events like the Gulf War also affected tourism earlier. It has been seen from experience that normally, major disruption from such events continue for one or two years before markets settle again to predictable growth pattern.

The WTO also draws on the past experience to derive lessons for the future and concludes on a optimistic note:[2] -

"Two of the major armed conflicts of the 1990s – the Gulf War in 1991 and the Kosovo conflict in 1999 – although they are only partially comparable with the current situation, triggerd a significant showdown in tourism growth, but not a fall-off in total arrivals. It should be noted that these types of movements have been followed by major growth in subsequent years; hence in 1991 (the year of the Gulf war) international tourism grew by 1.2 percent and in 1992 by 8.3 percent; in 1999 (the year of the Kosovoa conflict) international tourism rose by 3.8 percent.and in 2000 by 7.4 percent. The figures for both years also attest to the following trends:

- tourists avoided the aeas involved in the conflicts and those perceived as being too close at hand;

- there was a clear drop in interregional traffic, for example in 1999 tourism from the Americas to Europe fell 1.2 percent while total outbound tourism for the region grew by 1.6 percent;

- there ws a 'shift' effect to alternative destinations, particularly those within the region or within the tourist's country of residence.

However, everyone agrees that the earlier experiences were qualitatively slightly different from the present one. The primary effect this time will fall on demand for outbound international travel generally resulting from the effects of the events in the U.S. and from the effects of psychological fear regarding air travel. The earlier incidents mostly affected destination choice and the impact was mostly local. There is, therefore, a qualitative difference between the two situations.

A subsequent analysis by the Travel Business Round Table on 10th of October showed that traveller confidence was slow in returning inspite of various measures taken to boost up confidence. Mr. Tisch, Chairman of TBR cautioned against a sense of fals security and referred to disturbing trends following from lack of public confidence and the uncertainty about the impact of US action against terrorism on the world economy. Every one believes that hard decisions are required in exceptional situations like the present one. The impact on the travel and tourism industry in USA would affect the economic recovery as well. Before September 11, travel and tourism was the third largest US retail industry with $582 billion in revenue and workforce of more than 17 million people in 2000. It was America's second largest service export responsible for $17 billion trade surplus, and generating nearly $ 100 billion on Federal, State and local tax revenues. In the three weeks after September 11 more than 130,000 airline and aircraft manufacturing employees reportedly lost their jobs and the hotel industry has projected loss of nearly $2 billion in 2001 [TBR Review].

In the overlall general optimism about a quick recovery, there are many disturbing forebodings. Mr. Kofi Annan in his Address to the General Assembly referred to the thesis of a "clash of civilizations" according to which the world faces a Century of conflict between people of different faiths and cultures. Mr. Annan made a clarion call to fight against any such clash and to enrich culture by dialogue among civilizations. However, such a clash is seen by many as a reality unfolding. Imtiaz Muqbil, Executive Editor of Travel Impact Newswire in its edition of 11th October says "An industry that has prided itself on its cultural diversity and strengths, and long cited these as a contributor to global peace, is now under significant threat because of the looming clash."

The WTO report also indirectly refers to the dangerous and undesirable possibility of such a development.

According to the WTO analysis, some of the possible scenarios in such a situation could be[3] -

1. Strength of tourism demand and its resistance to crises.

2. Capacity of travel and tourism industry to overcome adverse situations endangeved by political and other crises.

3. In – built compensation phenomena whereby travellers tend to switch destination.

4. Possible scenario of a redistribution of overall demand with emergence of regional or domestic tourism.

5. More impact on long-haul journeys and, therefore, increasing shorter-haul journeys.

6. Air transport likely to be more affected and, therefore, areas dependent on other modes of transport likely to benefit.

On the basis of its general assessment and the possible scenarios, the WTO decided to maintain the annual average growth rate earlier predicted by it. The Organisation stands by its projections in the Tourism 2020 Vision. However, it suggests that every country should adopt professional, systematic and transparent measures to tackle the crises. The crisis period also is a period of rebuilding as it is shown by the success of

"The Amazing Thailand" campaign launched during the financial crisis management in a professional manner "The negative impact of a crisis faced by the country. WTO recommends crisis situation on a specific destination is generally conditioned by the way in which such crisis are handled. Broadly speaking, the impact can be scaled down by treating the matter in-

(1) an open transparent manner, notably with a view to the media and the big tour operators; and

(2) tackling problems professionally rather than trying to deny their existence.

This type of crisis management comprises actions related to specific public relations, promotion, communication and marketing campaigns." The PATA report[4] also recommends the following specific measures-

(a) shift market orientation and product offering

(b) aggressive promotion in select markets

(c) improve cross-industry and cross-national cooperation.

(d) lobby national government for support.

It is very clear that it is a time for more and not less tourism. Even in the best of times, tourism suffer for lack of coordination among all the players. In this situation of crisis , need for positive government actions is even more important.

Reference:

1. T.B.R. Report dated October 5, 2001.
2. W.T.O. The impact of the attacks in the United States on international tourism : an initial analysis.p.5.
3. W.T.O. op. cit. p. 5.
4. STRATFOR Special report prepared for PATA Bangkok – "The Post September 11 outlook for travel and Tourism in Asia and the pacific." October 14, 2001.

APPENDICES

Appendix- I

ECOTOURISM IN INDIA-POLICY AND GUIDELINES

1. ECOTOURISM : DEFINITION

The activities of persons travelling to and staying in places outside their usual place of residence for not more than one consecutive year for leisure, business and other purposes constitute tourism. Such visits for being close to nature to enjoy its enormous creations, both biotic and abiotic, in a most environment-friendly manner, without any adverse impact on the ecosystem, is particularly known as ecotourism.

According to the World Tourism Organisation (WTO), "tourism that involves travelling to relatively undisturbed natural areas with the specified object of studying, admiring and enjoying the scenery and its wild plants and animals, as well as any existing cultural aspects (both of the past or the present) found in these areas" is defined as ecotourism. Nature tourism (ecotourism) is distinguished from mass tourism or resort tourism by having a lower impact on the environment and by requiring less infrastructure development.

The key elements of ecotourism include a natural

environment as the prime attraction, an optimum number of environment-friendly visitors, activities which do not have any serious impact on the ecosystem and the positive involvement of the local community in maintaining the ecological balance.

Ecotourism can take many forms and magnitudes. For example, 'losing' oneself in a beautiful natural forest or landscape - watching animals, birds and trees in a forest, corals and marine life in sea, engaging in trekking, boating or rafting, wandering amongst sand dunes - these are some of the common forms of ecotourism.

Though the concept has gained importance only recently, India has been experiencing various forms of ecotourism all through the ages.

2. ECOTOURISM RESOURCES OF INDIA

The geographical diversity of India is a wealth of ecosystems which are well protected and preserved. These ecosystems have become the major resource for ecotourism in India.
They are :

1. Biosphere Reserves
2. Mangroves
3. Coral Reefs
4. Deserts
5. Mountains and Forests
6. Flora and Fauna
7. Seas, Lakes and Rivers
8. Caves

2.1. BIOSPHERE RESERVES

Biosphere reserves are multipurpose protected areas, for preservation of the genetic diversity and integrity of plants, animals and micro-organisms in representative ecosystems. There are seven such reserves in India at present :

(i) Nilgiri
(ii) Nanda Devi
(iii) Nokrek
(iv) Great Nicobar
(v) Gulf of Mannar
(vi) Manas
(vii) Sunderbans

2.2. MANGROVES

Mangroves are very specialised forest ecosystems of tropical and subtropical regions bordering sheltered sea coasts and estuaries.

Major mangroves areas are :

(i) Northern Andaman and Nicobar Islands
(ii) Sunderbans (West Bengal)
(iii) Bhitarkanika and Mahanadi Delta (Orissa)
(iv) Coringa, Godavari Delta and Krishna Estuary (Andhra Pradesh)
(v) Pichavaram and Point Calimere (Tamil Nadu)
(vi) Goa
(vii) Gulf of Kutch (Gujarat)
(viii) Coondapur (Karnataka)
(ix) Achra/Ratnagiri (Maharashtra)
(x) Vembanad (Kerala)

2.3 CORAL REEFS

There are four major coral reefs identified in the country so far :

(i) Gulf of Mannar
(ii) Andaman and Nicobar Islands
(iii) Lakshadweep Islands
(iv) Gulf of Kutch.

2.4. DESERTS

The Great Thar desert and the little deserts in the North Western Region of the country are distinct ecosystems which have fascinated tourists from all over the world.

2.5. MOUNTAINS AND FORESTS

The great Himalayas and other mountain ranges in the country, along with the snow-clad slopes, forests and rivers, have also become great attractions for ecotourists. The country has an area of about 752.3 lakh hectares notified as forest land and of this about 406.1 lakh hectares are classified as Reserve Forests and 215.1 lakh hectares as Protected Forests.

2.6. FLORA AND FAUNA

India is floristically very rich. She has about 45,000 species of plants. The country also has a great variety of fauna, numbering a little over 65,000 known species, including 1,228 of birds, 428 of reptiles, 372 of mammals, 204 of amphibians and 2,546 of fish.

In order to protect and preserve these genetic constituents, India has created a number of National Parks and 421 Wildlife Sanctuaries in different parts of the country. Some of these which have already become popular with tourists are Kaziranga and Manas in Assam; Jim Corbett in Uttar Pradesh; Keoladeo Ghana, Ranthambore and Sariska in Rajasthan; Kanha and Bandhavgarh in Madhya Pradesh; Bandipur in Karnataka and Simlipal in Orissa.

2.7. WATER RESOURCES

The Arabian Sea, the Indian Ocean and the Bay of Bengal brace the sides of the Indian subcontinent except for the northern boundary. The land mass of India is crossed by several rivers and dotted by lakes at many places. These water bodies provide attractive opportunities for watersports.

3. POLICY AND PLANNING

The national policy on tourism stipulates that tourism should become a unifying force nationally and internationally, fostering better understanding through travel.

It should also help to preserve, retain and enrich our world-view and life-style, our cultural expressions and heritage in all its manifestations. The prosperity that tourism brings should strengthen and cause accretion, rather than damage, to our social and cultural values and depletion of our natural resources.

Realisation of these policy objectives particularly in the context of ecotourism would involve a selective approach, scientific planning, effective control and continuous monitoring. The developmental process itself should meet the following cardinal principles :

(i) It should involve the local community and lead to the overall economic development of the area.

(ii) It should identify the likely conflicts between resource use for tourism and the livelihood of local inhabitants and attempt to minimise such conflicts.

(iii) The type and scale of tourism development should be compatible with the environment and sociocultural characteristics of the local community

(iv) It should be planned as a part of the overall area development strategy, guided by an integrated land-use plan and associated with commensurate expansion of public services.

The biospheres, mangroves, coral reefs, deserts and mountains which form the core resources for ecotourism, are fragile ecosystems. Hence decisions for the development of tourism in such areas have to be based on a thorough understanding of local resources, social and economic factors and other characteristics.

The objectives of tourism development in any specified area, as well as the intended beneficiaries, dependency and scale of development have to be decided on the basis of these factors and discussions and negotiations with those most directly concerned.

The development of physical infrastructure for tourism should be preceded by the preparation of an inventory of resources and a zoning/ management plan to ensure preservation and public use of valuable natural sites.

Whenever destruction or serious alteration of areas of high primary productivity like wetland, seagrass beds, coral reefs or rainforests is contemplated, benefits and costs should be carefully assessed before planning tourism development activities. Further, planning and promotion of tourism should be undertaken as a component part of an integrated, comprehensive resource management plan founded on sound ecological principles.

The Tourism Management Plan should also establish standards for resort development, covering among others, the style and locations of structures, treatment of sewage and control of litter, preservation of open spaces and public use of fragile areas. It should further lay down procedures to ensure that sewage is not directed to the beach or the ground water and solid waste is systematically collected and disposed of suitably. Adequate precautionary measures should also be taken to avoid noise pollution. It should also specify methods and material for construction activities and minimise any possible adverse impact on local environment.

Physical planning and design should integrate community services including availability of potable water, transportation and tourism. Transportation and access should also be integrated with other purposes such as industry and trade as communities are the termini for air, land and water access. Physical planning for all travel modes, especially modern tour buses, also needs to be integrated between segments outside and inside the area of attraction.

4. OPERATIONAL GUIDELINES

The key players in the ecotourism business are the Government, both Central and at State levels, the local authorities, the developers and the operators, the visitors and the local community. Each one of them has to be sensitive to the environment and local traditions and follow a set of guidelines for the successful development of tourism. In addition, non-governmental organisations and scientific/research institutions also have to play a key role in the development of ecotourism.

4.1 THE GOVERNMENT

* The Management Plan for each area should be prepared by professional landscape architects and urban planners, in consultation with the local

community as well as others directly concerned.

* Integrated planning should be adopted to avoid inter-sectoral and cross-sectoral conflict.

* The architectural programme for ecotourism centres should include controlled access points and cabins, roads, self-guided nature trails, transportation options, interpretive centres, signs, observation towers and blinds, adequate but unpretentious lodging and dining facilities, docks, garbage disposal facility and other utilities as per requirement. If needed, suitable living quarters and facilities for project personnel have to be provided.

* Structures creating visual pollution, unaesthetic values and non-compatible architecture, should be controlled and temporary structures using local building material and befitting the local environment should be encouraged.

* Exclude developments in geologically unstable zones and define development and buffer zones after proper environmental impact assessments.

* Establish standards, building codes and other regulations.

* Specify environmental, physical and social carrying capacities to limit development activities.

* Ensure continuous monitoring of adverse effects

of tourism activities and initiate suitable corrective measures.

* Recognise and award quality labels to ecotourism operators.

* Provide visitor information and interpretation services covering particularly—(i) what to see, (ii) how to see, (iii) how to behave. It can be by way of brochures, leaflets, specialised guides, visitor information centres and such.

* Prepare and widely distribute codes of conduct to all visitors.

* Launch training programmes on ecotourism to tourism administrators, planners, operators and general public.

4.2 DEVELOPERS, OPERATORS AND SUPPLIERS

v Respect and follow the planning restrictions, standards and codes provided by the government and local authorities.

v Implement sound environment principles through self-regulation.

v Practice environmental impact assessment for all new projects and conduct regular environmental audit for all ongoing activities leading to development of environmental improvement programmes.

- v Be sensitive to conservation of environmentally protected or threatened areas, species and scenic aesthetics, achieving landscape enhancement wherever possible.

- v Ensure that all structures are unobtrusive and do not interfere with the natural ecosystem to the maximum extent.
- v Recognise the optimal environmental capacity and sociological use-limits of the site in creating tourist facilities. They should also take into account safety and convenience of tourists.

- v Buildings should be designed strictly on functional and environmental considerations and avoid overconstruction.

- v Local material and designs should be used in all construction to the extent possible.

- v Physical planning, architectural design and construction of tourist facilities should employ ecofriendly techniques like solar energy, capture and utilisation of rain water, recycling of garbage, natural cross-ventilation instead of air-conditioning, a high level of self-sufficiency in food generation through orchards, ecological farms, aquaculture and such.

- v Energy and water-saving practices should be employed to the extent possible. Fresh water management and controlled sewage disposal should also be practised.

- Control air emissions—both chemical pollutants and noise.
- Control and reduce environmentally unfriendly products such as asbestos, CFCs, pesticides and toxic, corrosive, infectious, explosive or flammable material.
- Respect and support historic or religious objects and sites.
- Provide information and interpretive services to visitors especially on attractions and facilities, safety and security, local customs and traditions, prohibitions and regulations and self-conduct and behaviour.
- Ensure adequate opportunities to visitors for communion with nature and native cultures.
- In marketing ecotourism products, customers should be given correct information, as the visitors who appreciate ecotourism products usually belong to environmentally-aware groups.
- Training and research programmes of the company should, include environmental issues.
- Prepare tourists to minimise possible negative impact while visiting sensitive environments and cultures before their visit.
- Ensure safety and security of visitors and inform

them of precautions to be taken.

- Exercise due regard for the interest of the local population, including their history, tradition and culture and future economic development.

- Involve the local community to the extent possible in various activities and vocations.

4.3. THE VISITORS

- Help conserve habitats of flora and fauna and any site, natural or cultural, which may be affected by tourism.

- Make no open fires and discourage others from doing so. If water has to be heated with scarce firewood, use as little as possible. Where feasible, use kerosene or fuel-efficient wood stoves.

- Remove litter, burn or bury paper, and carry back all nondegradable litter.

- Keep local water clean and avoid using pollutants such as detergents in streams or springs. If no toilet facilities are available, try to relieve yourself at least 30 metres away from water sources and bury or cover the waste.

- Plants should be left to flourish in their natural environment and avoid taking away cuttings, seeds and roots.

- Leave the camp sites clean after use.

Remember that another party will be using the same camp site after your departure.

- v Help guides and porters to follow conservation measures. Do not allow cooks/porters to throw garbage in streams or rivers.

- v Respect the natural and cultural heritage of the area and follow local customs.
- v Respect local etiquette and wear loose clothes. Kissing in public is disapproved of.

- v Respect holy places—do not touch or remove religious objects.

- v Strictly follow the guidelines for personal safety and security and always take your own precautions and safety measures.

4.4. THE DESTINATION POPULATION/HOST COMMUNITY

- v Realise and respect the value of the environment, the flora and fauna, the monuments and the cultural heritage.

- v Practise conservation of nature and culture as a way of life.

- v Establish guidelines to protect valuable local resources and foster tourism management.

- v Realise and react to the potential threat of investors who see opportunities in development but lack sensitivity to local values.

- v Become effective nature guides and conservationists of natural areas by enhancing the practical and ancestral knowledge of the natural features of the area.

- v Be friendly with the visitors and help them to practise ecotourism codes.

4.5. NON-GOVERNMENTAL ORGANISATIONS/ SCIENTIFIC AND RESEARCH INSTITUTIONS

- v Create awareness, amongst all concerned, about the importance of sound ecopractices in tourism development.

- v Motivate the local community to increase their involvement in sustainable tourism activities.

- v Organise training programmes to prepare the local people for taking up various vocations relating to ecotourism.

THE ENVIRONMENTAL PLEDGE

1. ***Stationery and Other Publicity Material on Recycled Paper*** : We will introduce the use of recycled paper for our stationery and other publicity items such as brochures and establish a recycling programme.

2. ***Polythene Bags*** : We will convert, wherever possible, from the use of polythene bags to paper bags, cloth bags and other alternatives.

3. ***Alternate Source of Energy for Fuel*** : Where possible, we will convert to solar power such as solar heating and lighting, to reduce the use of thermal electricity.

4. ***Garbage Disposal*** : We will introduce the system of separating recyclable and non-recyclable garbage emanating from our operations and dispose non-biodegradable garbage in a responsible way, so as to not harm the environment.

5. ***Water Catchment and Treatment*** : Wherever possible, we will recycle water by incorporating water treatment schemes. We will also make storage and catchment facilities for rain water to be used for our operations.

6. ***Ecolodges and Resorts*** : We pledge to conserve the ecology, animal and birdlife of the area our properties are located in.

7. ***Planting of Saplings*** : We will encourage the planting of saplings and greening of the local environment.

8. ***Alternate Use of Fuels*** : We will limit the burning of firewood and use alternate sources of fuel for both cooking and leating.

9. ***Use of Local Ethnic Materials in Construction of Properties*** : In keeping with the local landscaping, we will incorporate architectural styles typical to the area, thus blending with the environment.

10. ***Employment of Local Communities*** : Wherever possible, we will hire locally for our business, to enhance the economy of our area.

11. ***Limit Deforestration*** : We will make no open fires and discourage others from doing so. Wherever water is heated using scarce firewood.,We will be not use it or use as little of it as possible. Wherever possible, we will choose accommodation that uses kerosene or fuel-efficient firewood stoves.

12. ***Plant Saplings*** : We will take saplings and encourage our tourists to hclp plant them near our camp sites or on the trails.

13. ***Non-Biodegradable Garbage*** : We will leave campsites clean and take back all non-biodegradable litter to the roadhead towns for proper disposal. We will bury only biodegradable food waste.

14. ***Keep Local Water Clean*** : Toilet facilities will be pitched at least 30 metres away from the water source and all waste will be covered

properly. We will not allow detergents to be used in streams and springs.

15. ***Plants lejt in their natural environment*** : We will not take away cuttings, seeds and roots-this is illegal in most parts of the Himalayas.

16. ***Respect Local Cultures*** : We will promote the appreciation and preservation of religious places and local villages by never allowing clients to buy religious objects or heirlooms from remote villages.

17. ***Alternate Source of Energy For Fuel*** : Where possible, we will convert to solar power such as solar lanterns and solar cookers.

Appendix II

Rio Declaration on Environment and Development

Having met at Rio de Janeiro from 3 to 14 June 1992,

Reaffirming the Declaration of the United Nations Conference on the Human Environment, adopted at Stockholm on 16 June 1972,[a] and seeking to build upon it,

With the goal of establishing a new and equitable global partnership through the creation of new levels of cooperation among States, key sectors of societies and people,

Working towards international agreements which respect the interests of all and protect the integrity of the global environmental and developmental system,

Recognizing the integral and interdependent nature of the Earth, our home,

Proclaims that:

PRINCIPLE 1

Human beings are at the centre of concerns for sustainable development. They are entitled to a healthy and productive life in harmony with nature.

PRINCIPLE 2

States have, in accordance with the Charter of the United Nations and the principles of international law, the sovereign right to exploit their own resources pursuant to their own environmental and developmental policies, and the responsibility to ensure that activities within their jurisdiction or control do not cause damage to the environment of other States or of areas beyond the limits of national jurisdiction.

PRINCIPLE 3

The right to development must be fulfilled so as to equitably meet developmental and environmental needs of present and future generations.

PRINCIPLE 4

In order to achieve sustainable development, environmental protection shall constitute an integral part of the development process and cannot be considered in isolation from it.

PRINCIPLE 5

All States and all people shall cooperate in the essential task of eradicating poverty as an indispensable requirement for sustainable development, in order to decrease the disparities in standards of living and better meet the needs of the majority of the people of the world.

PRINCIPLE 6

The special situation and needs of developing countries, particularly the least developed and those most environmentally vulnerable, shall be given special priority. International actions in the field of environment and development should also address the interests and needs of all countries.

PRINCIPLE 7

States shall cooperate in a spirit of global partnership to conserve, protect and restore the health and integrity of the Earth's ecosystem. In view of the different contributions to global environmental degradation. States have common but differentiated responsibilities. The developed countries acknowledge the responsibility that they bear in the international pursuit of sustainable development in view of the pressures their societies place on the global environment and of the technologies and financial resources they command.

PRINCIPLE 8

To achieve sustainable development and a higher quality of life for all people, States should reduce and eliminate unsustainable patterns of production and consumption and promote appropriate demographic policies.

PRINCIPLE 9

States should cooperate to strengthen endogenous capacity-building for sustainable development by improving scientific understanding through exchanges of scientific and technological knowledge, and by enhancing the development, adaptation, diffusion and transfer of technologies, including new and innovative technologies.

PRINCIPLE 10

Environmental issues are best handled with the participation of all concerned citizens, at the relevant level. At the national level, each individual shall have appropriate access to information concerning the environment that is held by public authorities, including information on hazardous materials and activities in their communities, and the opportunity to participate in decision-making processes. States shall facilitate and encourage public awareness and participation by making information widely available. Effective access to judicial and administrative proceedings, including redress and remedy, shall be provided.

PRINCIPLE 11

States shall enact effective environmental legislation. Environmental standards, management objectives and priorities should reflect the environmental and developmental context to which they apply. Standards applied by some countries may be inappropriate and of unwarranted economic and social cost to other countries, in particular developing countries.

PRINCIPLE 12

States should cooperate to promote a supportive and open international economic system that would lead to economic growth and sustainable development in all countries, to better address the problems of environmental degradation. Trade policy measures for environmental purposes should not constitute a means of arbitrary or unjustifiable discrimination or a disguised restriction on international trade. Unilateral actions to deal with environmental challenges outside the jurisdiction of the importing country should be avoided. Environmental measures addressing transboundary or global environmental problems should, as far as possible, be based on an international consensus.

PRINCIPLE 13

States shall develop national law regarding liability and compensation for the victims of pollution and other environmental damage. States shall also cooperate in an expeditious and more determined manner to develop further international law regarding liability and compensation for adverse effects of environmental damage caused by activities within their jurisdiction or control to areas beyond their jurisdiction.

PRINCIPLE 14

States should effectively cooperate to discourage or prevent the relocation and transfer to other States of any activities and substances that cause severe environmental degradation or are found to be harmful to human health.

PRINCIPLE 15

In order to protect the environment, the precautionary approach shall be widely applied by States according to their capabilities. Where there are threats of serious or irreversible damage, lack of full scientific certainty shall not be used as a reason for postponing cost-effective measures to prevent environmental degradation.

PRINCIPLE 16

National authorities should endeavour to promote the internalization of environmental costs and the use of economic instruments, taking into account the approach that the polluter should, in principle, bear the cost of pollution, with due regard to the public interest and without distorting international trade and investment.

PRINCIPLE 17

Environmental impact assessment, as a national instrument, shall be undertaken for proposed activities that are likely to have a significant adverse impact on the environment and are subject to a decision of a competent national authority.

PRINCIPLE 18

States shall immediately notify other States of any natural disasters or other emergencies that are likely to produce sudden harmful effects on the environment of those States. Every effort shall be made by the international community to help States so afflicted.

PRINCIPLE 19

States shall provide prior and timely notification and relevant information to potentially affected States on activities that may have a significant adverse transboundary environmental effect and shall consult with those States at an early stage and in good faith.

PRINCIPLE 20

Women have a vital role in environmental management and development. Their full participation is therefore essential to achieve sustainable development.

PRINCIPLE 21

The creativity, ideals and courage of the youth of the world should be mobilized to forge a global partnership in order to achieve sustainable development and ensure a better future for all.

PRINCIPLE 22

Indigenous people and their communities and other local communities have a vital role in environmental management and development because of their knowledge and traditional practices. States should recognize and duly support their identity, culture and interests and enable their effective participation in the achievement of sustainable development.

PRINCIPLE 23

The environment and natural resources of people under oppression, domination and occupation shall be protected.

PRINCIPLE 24

Warfare is inherently destructive of sustainable development. States shall therefore respect international law providing protection for the environment in times of armed conflict and cooperate in its further development, as necessary.

PRINCIPLE 25

Peace, development and environmental protection are interdependent and indivisible.

PRINCIPLE 26

States shall resolve all their environmental disputes peacefully and by appropriate means in accordance with the Charter of the United Nations.

PRINCIPLE 27

States and people shall cooperate in good faith and in a spirit of partnership in the fulfilment of the principles embodied in this Declaration and in the further development of international law in the field of sustainable development.

Appendix-III

Global Code of Ethics For Tourism

PREAMBLE

We, Members of the World Tourism Organization gathered for the General Assembly at Santiago, Chile on this first day of October 1999,

Reasserting the aims set out in Article 3 of the Statutes of the World Tourism Organization, and aware of the "decisive and central" role of this Organization, as recognized by the General Assembly of the United Nations, in promoting and developing tourism with a view to contributing to economic development, international understanding, peace, prosperity and universal respect for and observation of, human rights and fundamental freedoms for all without distinction as to race, sex, language or religion,

Firmly believing that, through the direct, spontaneous and non-mediatized contacts it engenders between men and women of different cultures and lifestyles, tourism factor of friendship and understanding among the peoples of the world,

In keeping with the rationale of reconciling environmental protection, economic development and the fight against poverty in a sustainable manner, as formulated by the United Nations in 1992 at the "Earth Summit" of Rio de Janeiro and expressed in Agenda 21, adopted on that occasion,

Taking into account the swift and continued growth, both past and foreseeable, of the tourism activity, whether for leisure, business, culture, religious or health purposes, and its powerful effects, both positive and negative, on the environment, the economy and the society of both generating and receiving countries, on local communities and indigenous peoples, as well as on international relations and trade,

Aiming to promote responsible, sustainable and universally accessible tourism in the framework of the right of all persons to use their free time for leisure pursuits or travel with respect for the choices of society of all peoples,

But convinced that the world tourism industry as a whole has much to gain by operating in an environment that favours the market economy, private enterprise and free trade and that serves to optimize its beneficial effects on the creation of wealth and employment,

Also firmly convinced that, provided a number

of principles and a certain number of rules are observed, responsible and sustainable tourism is by no means incompatible with the growing liberalization of' the condition governing trade in services and under whose aegis the enterprises of' this sector operate and that it is possible to reconcile in this sector economy and ecology, environment and development. openness to international trade and protection of social and cultural identities,

Considering that, with such an approach, all the stakeholders 'in tourism development - national, regional and local administrations, enterprises, business associations, workers in the sector non-governmental organizations and bodies of all kinds belonging to the tourism industry, as well as host communities, the media and the tourists themselves, have different albeit interdependent responsibilities in the individual and societal development of tourism and that the formulation of their individual rights and duties will contribute to meeting this aim,

Committed, in keeping with the aims pursued by the World Tourism Organization itself since adopting resolution 364 (XII) at its General Assembly of 1997 (Istanbul), to promote a genuine partnership between 'the public and private stakeholders in tourism development, and wishing to see a partnership and cooperation of the same kind extend, in an open and balanced way, to the relations between generating and receiving countries and their respective tourism industries,

Following up on the Manila Declaration of 1980 on World Tourism and of 1997 on the Social Impact of Tourism, as well as on the Tourism Bill of Rights and the Tourist Code adopted at Sofia in 1985 under the aegis of WTO,

But believing that these instruments should be complemented by a set of interdependent principles for their interpretation and application on which the stakeholders in tourism development should model their conduct at the dawn of the twenty-first century,

Using, for the purposes of this instrument, the definitions and classifications applicable to travel, and especially the concepts of "Visitor", "tourist" and "tourism", as adopted by the Ottawa International Conference, held from 24 to 28 June 1991 and approved, in 1993, by the United Nations Statistical Commission and at its twenty-seventh session,

Referring in particular to the following instruments:

Universal Declaration of Human Rights of 10 December 1948;

- International Covenant on Economic, Social and Cultural Rights of 16 December 1966;
- International Covenant on Civil and Political Rights of 16 December 1966;
- 0 Warsaw Convention on Air Transport of 12 October 1929;

- Chicago Convention on International Civil Aviation of 7 December 1944, and the Tokyo, The Hague and Montreal Convention in relation thereto;

- Convention on Customs Facilities for - Tourism of 4 July 1954 and related Protocol,
- Convention concerning the Protection of the World Cultural and Natural Heritage of 23 November 1972;

- Manila Declaration on World

- Tourism of 10 October 1980;

- Resolution of the Sixth General, Assembly of WTO (Sofia) adopting the Tourism Bill of Rights and Tourist Code of' 26 September 1985;

- Convention on the Rights of the Child of 26 January 1990;

- Resolution of' the Ninth General Assembly of WTO (Buenos Aires) concerning in particular travel facilitation and the safety and security of tourists of' 4 October 1991;

- Rio Declaration on the Environment and Development of 13 June 1992;

- General Agreement on Trade in Services of 15 April 1994 Convention on Biodiversity of 6 January 1995;

- Resolution of the Eleventh General Assembly of WTO (Cairo) on the prevention of organized sex tourism of 22 October 1995;

- Stockholm Declaration of 28 August 1996 against the Commercial Sexual Exploitation of Children;

- Manila Declaration on the Social Impact of Tourism of 22 May 1997;

- Conventions and recommendations adopted by the International Labour Organisation in the area of collective conventions, prohibition of forced labour and child labour, defence of the rights of indigenous peoples, and equal treatment and non-discrimination in the work place;

affirm the right to tourism and the freedom of tourist movements,

state our wish to promote an equitable, responsible and sustainable world tourism order, whose benefits will be shared by all sectors of society in the context of an open and liberalized international economy, and solemnly adopt to these ends the principles of the *Global Code of* ***Ethics for Tourism.***

1. ***Tourism's contribution to mutual understanding and respect between peoples and societies***

1. The understanding and promotion of' the ethical values common to humanity with an attitude of tolerance and respect for the diversity of religious, philosophical and moral beliefs, are both the foundation and the consequence of' responsible tourism; stakeholders in tourism development and tourists themselves should observe the social and cultural traditions and practices of all peoples, including those of' minorities and indigenous peoples and to recognized their worth;

2. Tourism activities should be conducted in harmony with the attributes and tradition of the host regions and countries and in respect for their laws, practices and customs;

3. The host communities, on the one hand, and local professionals, on the other, should acquaint themselves with and respect the tourists who visit them and find out about their lifestyles, tastes and expectations; the education and training imparted to professionals contribute to a hospitable welcome;

4. It is the task of the public authorities to provide protection for tourists and visitors and their belongings; they must pay particular attention to the safety of foreign tourists owing to the particular vulnerability they may have; they should facilitate the introduction of specific means of information, prevention, security, insurance and assistance consistent with their needs; any attacks, assaults, kidnappings or threats against tourists or workers in the tourism industry, as well as the wilful destruction of tourism facilities or of elements of cultural or

natural heritage should be severely condemned and punished in accordance with their respective national laws;

5. When travelling, tourists and visitors should not commit any criminal act or any act considered criminal by the laws of the country visited and abstain from any conduct felt to be offensive or injurious by the local populations, or likely to damage the local environment; they should refrain from all trafficking in illicit drugs, arms, antiques, protected species and products and substances that are dangerous or prohibited by national regulations;

6. Tourist and visitors have the responsibility to acquaint themselves, even before their departure, with the characteristics of the countries they are preparing to visit; they must be aware of' the health and security risks inherent in any travel outside their usual environment and behave in such a way as to minimize those risks;

2. *Tourism as a vehicle for individual and collective fulfilment*

1. Tourism, the activity most frequently associated with rest and relaxation, sport and access to culture and nature, should be planned and practised as a privileged means of individual and collective fulfilment, when practised with a sufficiently open mind, it is an irreplaceable factor of self education, mutual tolerance and for learning about the legitimate differences between peoples and cultures and their diversity;

2. Tourism activities should respect the equality of men and women; they should promote human rights and, more particularly, the individual rights of the most vulnerable groups, notably children, the elderly, the handicapped, ethnic minorities and indigenous peoples;

3. The exploitation of human beings in any form, particularly sexual, especially when applied to children, conflicts with the fundamental aims of tourism and is the negation of' tourism; as such, in accordance with international law, it should be energetically combatted with the cooperation of all the States concerned and penalized without concession by the national legislation of both the countries visited and the countries of the perpetrators of these acts, even when they are carried out abroad;

4. Travel for purposes of religion, health, education and cultural or linguistic exchanges are particularly beneficial forms of tourism, which deserve encouragement;

5. The introduction into curricula of' education about the value of tourist exchanges, their economic, social and cultural benefits, and also their risks, should be encouraged;

3. *Tourism, a factor of sustainable development*

1. All the stakeholders in tourism development should safeguard the natural environment with a view to achieving sound, continuous and sustainable economic growth geared to satisfying equitably the

needs and aspirations of present and future generations;

2. All forms of tourism development that are conducive to saving rare and precious resources, in particular water and energy, as well as avoiding so far as possible waste production, should be given priority and encouraged by national, regional and local public authorities;

3. The staggering in time and space of' tourist and visitor flows, particularly those resulting from paid leave and school holidays, and a more even distribution of holidays should he sought so as to reduce the pressure of' tourism activity on the environment and enhance its beneficial impact on the tourism industry and the local economy;

4. Tourism infrastructure should be designed and tourism activities programmed in such a way as to protect the natural heritage composed of ecosystems and biodiversity and to preserve endangered species of wildlife; the stakeholders in tourism development, and especially professionals, should agree to the imposition of limitations or constraints on their activities when these are exercised in particularly sensitive areas: desert, polar or high mountain regions, coastal areas, tropical forests or wetlands, propitious to the creation of nature reserves or protected areas;

5. Nature tourism and ecotourism are recognized as being particularly conducive to enriching and enhancing the standing of tourism, provided they

respect the natural heritage and local populations and are in keeping with the carrying capacity of the sites;

4. *Tourism, a user of the cultural heritage of mankind and a contributor to its enhancement*

1. Tourism resources belong to the common heritage of mankind; the communities in whose territories they are situated have particular rights and obligations to them;

2. Tourism policies and activities should be conducted with respect for the artistic, archaeological and cultural heritage, which they should protect and pass on to future generations; particular care should be devoted to preserving and upgrading monuments, shrines and museums as well as archaeological and historic sites which must be widely open to tourist visits; encouragement should be given to public access to privately-owned cultural property and monuments, with respect for the sights of their owners, as well as, to religious buildings without prejudice to normal needs of worship;

3. Financial resources derived from visits to cultural sites and monuments should, at least in part, be used for the upkeep, safeguard, development and embellishment of this heritage;

4. Tourism activity should be planned in such a way as to allow traditional cultural products, crafts and folklore to survive and flourish, rather than causing them to degenerate and become standardized;

5. *Tourism, a beneficial activity for host countries and communities*

1. Local populations should be associated with tourism activities and share equitably in the economic, social and cultural benefits they generate, and particularly in the creation of direct and indirect jobs resulting from them;

2. Tourism policies should he applied in such a way as to help to raise the standard of living of' the populations of the regions visited and meet their needs; the planning and architectural approach to and operation of tourism resorts and accommodation should aim to integrate them, to the extent possible, in the local economic and social fabric; where skills are equal, priority should be given to local manpower;

3. Special attention should be paid to the specific problems of' coastal areas and island territories and to vulnerable rural or mountain regions, for which tourism often represents a rare opportunity for development in the face of the decline of traditional economic activities;

4. Tourism professionals, particularly investors, governed by the regulations laid down by the public authorities, should carry out studies of the impact of their development projects on the environment and natural surroundings; they should also deliver, with the greatest transparency and objectivity, information on their future programmes and their foreseeable repercussions and foster dialogue on their contents

with the populations concerned;

6. *Obligations of stakeholders in tourism development*

1. Tourism professionals have an obligation to provide tourists with objective and honest information on their places of destination and on the conditions of travel, hospitality and stays; they should ensure that the contractual clauses proposed to their customers are readily understandable as to the nature, price and quality of the services they commit themselves to providing and the financial compensation payable by them in the event of a unilateral breach of contract on their part;

2. Tourism professionals, insofar as it depends on them, should show concern, in cooperation with the public authorities, for the security and safety, accident prevention; health protection and food safety of those who seek their services, likewise, they should ensure the existence of suitable systems of insurance and assistance; they should accept the reporting obligations prescribed by national regulations and pay fair compensation in the event of failure to observe; their contractual obligations;

3. Tourism professionals, so far as this depends on them, should contribute to the cultural and spiritual fulfilment of tourists and allow them, during their travels, to practice their religions;

4. The public authorities of the generating States and the host countries, in cooperation with the

professionals concerned and their associations, should ensure that the necessary mechanisms are in place for the repatriation of tourists in the event of the bankruptcy of the enterprise that organized their travel;

5. Governments have the right - and the duty - especially in a crisis, to inform their nationals of the difficult circumstances, or even the dangers they may encounter during their travels abroad; it is their responsibility however to issue such information without prejudicing in an unjustified or exaggerated manner the tourism industry of the host countries and the interests of their own operators; the contents of travel advisories should therefore be discussed beforehand with the authorities of the host countries and the professionals concerned; recommendations formulated should be strictly proportionate to the gravity of the situations encountered and confined to the geographical areas where the insecurity has arisen; such advisories should be qualified or cancelled as soon as a return to normality permits;

6. The press, and particularly the specialized travel press and the other media, including modern means of electronic communication, should issue honest and balanced information on events and situations that could influence the flow of tourists; they should also provide accurate and reliable information to the consumers of tourism services; the new communication and electronic commerce technologies should also be developed and used for this purpose; as is the case for the media, they should not in any way promote sex tourism;

7. ***Right to tourism***

1. The prospect of direct and personal access to the discovery and enjoyment of the Planet's resources constitutes a right equally open to all the world's inhabitants; the increasingly extensive participation in national and international tourism should be regarded as one of the best possible expressions of the sustained growth of free time, and obstacles should not be placed in its way;

2. The universal right to tourism must be regarded as the corollary of the right to rest and leisure, including reasonable limitation of working hours and periodic holidays with pay, guaranteed by Article 24 of the *Universal Declaration of Human Rights and Article 7.d of the International Covenant on Economic, Social and Cultural Rights*

3. Social tourism, and in particular associative tourism, which facilitates widespread access to leisure, travel and holidays, should be developed with the support of the public authorities;

4. Family, youth, student and senior tourism and tourism for people with disabilities, should be encouraged and facilitated,

8. ***Liberty of tourist movements***

1. Tourists and visitors should benefit, in compliance with international law and national legislation, from the liberty to move within their countries and from one State to another, in

accordance with Article 13 of the *Universal Declaration of Human Rights;* they should have access to places of transit and stay and to tourism and cultural sites without being subject to excessive formalities or discrimination;

2. Tourists and visitors should have access to all available forms of communication, internal or external; they should benifit from prompt and easy access to local administrative, legal and health services they should be free to contact the consular representatives of their countries of origin in compliance with the diplomatic conventions in force;

3. Tourists and visitors should benefit from the same rights as the citizens of the country visited concerning the confidentiality of the personal data and information concerning them, especially when these are stored electronically;

4. Administrative procedures relating, to border crossings whether they fall within the competence of States or result front international agreements, such as visas or health and customs formalities, should be adapted, so far as possible, so as to facilitate to the maximum freedom of travel and widespread access to international tourism; agreements between groups of countries to harmonize and simplify these procedures should be encouraged; specific taxes and levies penalizing the tourism industry and undermining its competitiveness should be gradually phased out or corrected;

5. So far as the economic situation of the countries

from which they come permits, travellers should have access to allowances of convertible currencies needed for their travels;

9. *Rights of the workers and entrepreneurs in the tourism industry*

1. The fundamental rights of salaried and self-employed workers in the tourism industry and related activities, should be guaranteed under the supervision of the national and local administrations, both of their States of origin and of the host countries with particular care, given the. specific constraints linked in particular to the seasonality of their activity, the global dimension of their industry and the flexibility often required of them by the nature of their work;

2. Salaried and self-employed workers in the tourism industry and related activities have the right and the duty to acquire appropriate initial and continuous training; they should be given adequate social protection; job insecurity should be limited so far as possible; and a specific status, with particular regard to their social welfare, should be offered to seasonal workers in the sector;

3. Any natural or legal person, provided he, she or it has the necessary abilities and skills, should be entitled to develop a professional activity in the field of tourism under existing national laws, enterpreneurs and investors-especially in the area of' small and medium-sized enterprises- should be entitled to free access to the tourism sector with a minimum of legal

or administrative restrictions;

4. Exchanges of experience offered to executives and workers, whether salaried or not, from different countries, contributes to foster the development of the world tourism industry; these movements should be facilitated so far as possible in compliance with the applicable national laws and international conventions;

5. As an irreplaceable factor of solidarity in the development and dynamic growth of international changes, multinational enterprises of the tourism industry should not exploit the dominant positions they sometimes occupy; they should avoid becoming the vehicles of cultural and social models artificially imposed on the host communities; in exchange for their freedom to invest and trade which should be fully recognized, they should involve themselves in local development, avoiding, by the excessive repatriation of their profits or their induced imports, a reduction of their contribution to the economies in which they are established;

6. Partnership and the establishment of balanced relations between enterprises of generating and receiving countries contribute to the sustainable development of tourism and an equitable distribution of the benefits of' its growth;

10. ***Implementation of the principles of Global Code of Ethics for Tourism***

1. The public and private stakeholders in tourism development should cooperate in the implementation

of these principles and monitor their effective application;

2. The stakeholders in tourism development should recognize the role of international institutions, among which the World Tourism Organization ranks first, and non-governmental organizations with competence in the field of tourism promotion and development, the protection of human rights, the environment or health, with due respect for the general principles of international law;

3. The same stakeholders should demonstrate their intention to refer any disputes concerning the application or interpretation of the Global Code of Ethics for Tourism for conciliation to an impartial third body known as the World Committee on Tourism Ethics.

Appendix-IV

EXTRACT FROM

ACTION PLAN FOR DEVELOPMENT OF TOURISM

RECOMMENDED BY

THE TASK FORCES

SET UP BY

MINISTRY OF TOURISM GOVERNMENT OF INDIA

SECTION : 1

Short - Term and Long - Term Action Plans

The recommendations made by Task Forces were considered by a Core Group comprising of representation of Central Ministries, Public Sector Undertakings, Private Associations and Tourism experts. The Composition of the Core Group is given at Annex - IV. In the light of the suggestions made by the Core Group, the recommendations were drafted into Short-Term and Long-Term Action Plans, achievable within one year and five year duration respectively. The lead agency that is responsible for execution and those concerned with it in the Public and Private Sectors have also been identified.

SHORT-TERM ACTION PLAN IMPLEMENTABLE WITHIN ONE YEAR

S.No.	Item	Lead Agency	Public Sector	Private Sector
1.	Place tourism high on the agenda of the nation	MOT MOEA, MOH PC, MOF		
2.	Declare Tourism as an Infrastructure Industry.	MOF, PC		

3.	Establish Tourism Promotion State Leaded Committees in each Governments State by the respective Chief Ministers.		
4.	Establish on Autonomous National Tourism Promotion Board.	MOT, PC, MOF	
5.	Allocate 30% of Expenditure Tax Collected to the Board.	MOF	
6.	Establish State Tourism Marketing Authorities for domestic tourism marketing.	MOT SG	
7.	Ensure that immigration officers are specially selected and fully trained.	MOH	IB
8.(i)	Undertake an immediate house Keeping drive at all the airports to ensure proper functioning of tourist facilities like air-conditions, coolers, fans, cold water, toilets, launges, etc.	MOCA	AAI
(ii)	A small committee need be set up to examine up-		

gradation of facilities at International Airports.			
9. Ensure Maximum Dwell Time of 45 mts for international arrivals and 60 mts for international departures.	MOCA	AAI	AL
10. Prepare and implement an action programme for more productive use of the existing capacities of Indian Airlines and Alliance Air.	MOCA	AI AAI IA AA	
11. Introduce attractive airfares with stop over privileges and minimum stay from 4 to 10 days from USA, Europe and Asia by Air India .	MOCA	AI	
12. Develop and market IA package tours covering important tourists centres.	MOCA	IA	IATO, TAAI
13. Introduce 'Inflight shops' in domestic airlines.	MOCA	IA AA	PA
14. Improve the customer care services by all the airlines and ensure exact flight information.	MOCA	AAI IA	PA

15.	International tourist/Foreign visitor channel for quick movements on arrival/ departure be instituted on single point central/check system.	MHA	AAI
16.	Booking facilitation counter and Cyber Cafe to be provided in the international Airport for providing on the spot Hotel and Transport Bookings.	MOCA MOT	AAI
17.	Provide uniforms to immigration staff.	MHA	
18.	Provide CCTV at International Airports to facilitate extensive monitoring. It should cover the entire area from Immigration to taxi pick up points.	MOCA	AAI
19.	Evolve a comprehensive package for improvement and upgradation of Airports. A Consultancy Agency be engaged for this purpose.	MOCA	AAI
20.	For efficient functioning of all services at the Airport, make the Airport Director excercise administratative control over	MHA MOF	AAI

	all agencies working in the premises. The technical and professional control could however vest with the concerned department/ agency.		
21.	The arrival hall in the immigration area to be improved and provided with proper facilities.	MOCA	AAI
22.	Provide proper lights on roads leading from International and Domestic Airports to the city.	SG	
23.	Enact laws to deal with the problems of Touting at the Airports.	SG	
24.	The printing of visa labels and issue of visas need to be fully computerised.	MOEA	
25.	Rescind the principle of reciprocity in visa regulations and relax them as follows : (i) No visa for the national of USA, European Union, UK and Japan.	MOH MOEA	

(ii) Availability of visa on arrival for the citizens of other friendly tourist generating countries.			
26. Introduce a system of combined air and rail bookings through Air India Sales Agents abroad.	Rlys MOCA		AISA
27. Disseminate information relating ro railways and rail tourism through websites, information centres/Kiosks, brouchers, user friendly timetables etc.	Rlys MOT	ITDS STDC	H,TA,TO
28. Promote National Railway Museum at Delhi as a tourist attraction.	MOT Rlys		
29. Utilise selected college/ School hostels during vacation for promoting youth and student tourism.	MOT SG	ITDC STDC	
30. Restrict the validity of guide licenses to two years and revalidate them only after successful completion of refresher courses.	MOT ASI		MOT

31. Evolve policies and programes for promoting partnerships between Archaeological survey of India and the private sector in the upkeep, management and marketing of monuments and muscums.	ASI MOT SG	IATO TAAI
32. Evolve an enabling environment for attracting private investment in the tourism sector. Some suggested measures are :		
(i) Exemption from Expenditure Tax all receipts in foreign exchange.	MOT MOF	
(ii) Limiting service tax only to those units not paying expenditure tax.		
(iii) Restrict excise duty on cakes/pastries only to packaged items sold through retail outlets.		
(iv) Restrict the Food and Beverage tax and luxury tax uniformly by all the states to 5% each and no luxury tax on payment made in foreign exchange.		

(v) Allow duty draw back on purchase of Indian manufactured items by foreign tourist at duty free shops.		
33. Modernise Duty free shops at the airports.	MOCA AAI	
34. Expedite the introdction of composite permit to tourist transport coaches/cars.	MOT MOST SG	
35. Rationalise, motor Vehicles tax.	MOST, MOT	
36. Set up a Special Committee to review all the existing systems, procedures and practices on processing of project proposals relating to tourism by various agencices and simplify them.	MOT MOF MOEF	
37. Carry out site assessement of World Heritage Centres and other major national monuments with a view to.	ASI MOT SG	INTACH
(i) Document the monuments including the existing state of preservation, damage, encroachement, etc. and		

	(ii) Prepare site management plans including repair and re-furbishment of monument, visitor facilities etc.		
38.	Set-up Monument Conservation Authorities Consisting of representatives of all types of Stake holders for important monuments.	ASI MOT SG	H,TA,TO TTO,OPF INTACH
39.	Major share of the entrance fee be utilized for the upkeep of the monuments and the area around them.	ASI MOT	
40.	Make accommodation units around wild life santuaries and National parks clean, hygienic and comfortable.	MOT MOEF SG	
41.	Commission case studies to assess the impact of tourism on employment and income generation in the local economy.	MOT SG	
42.	Integrate 'Time Share' holiday providers and Apartment hotels with tourism facilities and products.	MOT SG	TSA

43. Introduce a system for identification, approval and certification of 'Adventure Tourism Products' to assist the potential customers with quality products.	MOT SG	NIWS IISM	IATO TAAI
44. Indian Missions in major tourist generating countries to take up tourism promotion and visa services as mainstream activity.	MOEA MOT		
45. Establish on INTERNET PORTAL by the Ministry of Tourism so that all the tourism related webpages can be accessed from the same portal.	MOT SG MOCA ASI Rlys		TAAI,HAI IATO
46. Strengthen the National Institute of Water Sports and Indian Institute of Skiing and Mountaineering.	MOT MOF	NIWS IISM	
47. Introduce Management Development Programmes by the Indian Institute of Tourism and Travel Management (IITTM).	MOT	IITAM	

48. Set-up a National Tourism Documentation centre equipped with modern technology systems to function as a repository of research findings and publications on tourism.	MOT		
49. Institute Research Fellowships in selected universities and Indian Institute of Tourism and Travel Management (IITTM).	MOT	IITTM	
50. Establish proper institutional mechanisms for training and retraining of personnel at all points of tourist contact particularly immigration officials, porters, taxi drivers, guides, etc. with a view to enhance their knowledge, skills and attitudes.	MOT MOCA MOF MOH SG ASI	IITTM AAI	HAI IATO TAAI
51. Utilise new technolgical instruments like video tapes, CD-ROMS, etc. for training of service providers in tourism.	MOT SG	IITTAM AICTE	H,TA,TO TTO,OPF
52. Regulate the mushroom growth of training institutes in tourism and introduce quality certification of training.	MOT SG		

53. To set up a review committee for developing unified tourism course programme in the country.	MOT		
54. Introduce tourism in the school curriculum.	MOT,SG		
55. To develop mechanism for coordinating the individual activities/shows of ASSOCHAM, CII, FICCI Tourism Trade and the Government.	MOT SG	ITDC STDC	ASSO CHAM CII FICCI,HAI IATO TAAI
56. Sponsor Indian Food festivals, cultural shows, etc. along with Indian National Day celebrations of Indian High Commissions/Embassies in major tourist generating countries.	MOT MOEA		
57. Introduce international standard taxi services at all the airports. A separate class of Tourist Taxis for Airports including A/C cars to be introduced. These should have different colours, separate tarriff structure and radio communication facilities	MOST MOT SG	ITDC STDC	TAAI IATO

	and should not be older than 3 years to ensured quality. The taxi should display the name and photograph of driver, taxi number etc. inside.			
58.	Provide proper signages at the airports, railway stations, main bus and taxi stands and important road junctions.	MOCA Rlys. MOST MOT,SG	AAI	
59.	Organise airports parkings more conveniently and efficiently with proper traffic/ movement control.	MOCA. SG	AAI	IATO
60.	One taxi rank should be designated at the airport. The taxis should be properly queued up and regulated for picking up passengers.	SG		
61.	Evolve and implement marketing stategies based on market research and segmentation and monitor them continuously.	MOT MOEA	AI IA	H,TA,TO TTO,OPF
62.	Strengthen and improve market research and analysis so as to create technology oriented information systems.	MOT		

63. Produce road maps of important tourist centres for the international visitors.	MOST MOT		
64. To prepare India Tourist Atlas.	MOT	AI	TA,TO
65. Enhance overseas promotional and marketing budget.	MOT		
66. Introduce a CESS on the tourism industry as a percentage of turn over for market research and marketing.	MOF MOT		
67. Give wide publicity to Indian cuisine abroad.	MOT	AI	IATO
68. Achieve adequate co-ordination and synergy between promotional efforts of the Government, Air India, Indian Airlines and the Private Sector.	MOEA32.		

LONG-TERM CONDITION PLAN IMPLEMENTABLE WITHIN FIVE YEARS

S.No.	Item	Lead Agency	Public Sector	Private Sector
1.	Deploy Special Tourism Police Force at important tourist centres.	MOH SG		
2.	Provide money changing facilities at all the important airports, railway stations and tourist centres	RBI	Bank	H,TA,TO
3.	Establish Tourist Facilitation/Interpretation/ Information Centres, at the airports,important railway stations,tourist centres, monuments, etc.	MOT MOCA Rlys SG ASI	AAI ITDC STDC	
4.	Install category III Instrument Landing System at all the international airports.	MOCA	AAI	
5.	Increase revenue earnings from non-aeronautical services like restaurants, duty free shops, hotels, etc., to the international norms of about 60-70%.	MOCA	AAI	IATO HAI,TAAI

6.	Carry out a survey of the capabilities of all the airports and prepare and implement an action plan to provide the minimum tourist facilities in each of them.	MOCA MOT DGCA	AAI	
7.	Provide customs and immigration facilities at major airports for allowing international flights, particularly charter flights to operate freely.	MOCA MOH	AAI	
8.	Expedite the process of corporatisation of airports.	MOCA	AAI	
9.	Increase international air seat capacity to and from India by encouraging charter flights, rescinding the principle of reciprocity in bilateral air agreements and exposing an open sky strategy.	MOCA	AI	TAAI IATO
10.	Regional airlines with the air crafts of requisite size and specification need to be encouraged and the policy of route sharing between Indian Airlines and private	MOCA	IA AA PA	

	airlines should not become a burden for aspiring operators.			
11.	Introduce Air taxi services to major tourist centres.	MOCA	IA,AA, PA,	
12.	Introduce tourism oriented flight schedules with particular emphasis on high frequency coverage of tourist centres like Jodhpur, Udampur, Khajuraho, Aurangabad, etc. by Indian Airlines.	MOCA	IA AA	
13.	Improve/construct roadways in hight traffic route like the following :- Delhi-Jaipur-Udaipur Jodhpur-Jaisalmer Agra-Khajuraho Kalka-Shimla Chennai-Bangalore Bangalore-Mysore Chennai-Mahabalipuram Patna-Vaishali-Bodhgaya-Rajgir Patna-Rajgir-Nalanda Varanasi-Sarnath-Lumbini Gorakhpur-Kapilvastu-Lumbini-Sravasti	MOST SG		OPF

	Lucknow-Bairampur-Sravasti Bombay-Aurangabad-Ajanta-Ellora Kinnour-Sangla Valley-Tabo Monastory Dharamshala-Pangi-Leh.			
14.	Expedite four laning of busy national highway corridors.	MOST SG		
15.	Promote Multi-Modal Transport.	MOST SG		TA,TO
16.	Introduce special tourist trains with private sector participation in the following routes	Rlys SG	STDC	IATO ITTA
	(i) Delhi-Jaipur-Gwalior-Jhansi-Varanasi-Luknow-Delhi.			
	(ii) Bangalore-Mysore-Chennai-Kodaikanal-Kanya Kumari-Trivendrum-Cochin-Bangalaore.			
	(iii) Mumbai-Aurangabad-Nanded-Secunderabad-Hyderabad-Pune-Mumbai.			

	(iv) Calcutta-Gaya(Rajgir/ Nalanda)-Varanasi-Sarnath-Gorakhpur (Lumbini/ Kushinagar)-Calcutta.			
	(v) Hyderabad-Mantralayam-Dharamvarm-Puttaparto-Bangalore-Tirupati-Kalahasti-Guntur-Mancheral-Nadikudi-Hyderabad.			
	(vi) Chennai(Egmore)-Pondicherry-Nagore-Karaikal-Velankanni-Tiruchirappalli-Madurai-Rameswaram-Thanjavur-Chidambaram-Chennai.			
	(vii)Delhi-Bikaner-Shekhawati-Chittorgarh-Jaipur-Delhi.			
17.	Introduce A/C coach service/ Package tours in Major tourist circuits by the travel industry.	SG	STDC	IATO
18.	Establish Railway hotels at 100 nodes with private sector participation.	Rlys	ITDC STDC	HAI

19.	Maintain and market railway hertiage structure like Mumbai/VT/Mumbai/ Churchgate railway station, Lucknow railway station, Division Railway office at Ajmer and Railway hotels at Puri and Ranchi.	Rlys ASI SG	ITDC STDC	IATO TAAI
20	Convert hill railways enerypted by UNESCO as world heritage into attractive tourism products.	Rlys SG	ITDC STDC	IATO TAAI
21.	Maintain steam hauled tourist trains like Royal Orient, Buddha Parikrama, Fairy Queen, etc. in specific tourist sectors.	Rlys SG	ITDC STDC	IATO TAAI
22.	Introduce more Shatabdi and Rajadhani trains with special tourism and hospitablity focus.	Rlys	ITDC STDC	IATO
23.	Open up the tourist spots along the coastline for cruise tourism on the following routs : (i) Mumbai-Goa-Cochin (ii) Mumbai-Ratnagiri (iii) Calcutta-Puri	SG	SCI	IATO

	(iv) Chennai-Rameshwaram (v) Various points in the Brahamaputra (vi) Varanasi-Prayag (vii) Delhi-Allahabad (viii) Backwater-Tourism in Kerala (ix) Channai-Andaman (x) Calcutta-Andaman (xi) Hooghly-cruises			
24.	Introduce river and back water cruise as major tourist attraction in Brahmaputra.	MOT	IWAI	TA,TO
25.	Identify development zones for hotels and other tourism establishment in major tourist centres and ensure single window clearance of projects in such zones.	SG MOT		
26.	Ensure availability of land for expansion of hotel rooms by initiating the following steps (i) Make available more plots for hotel projects on easy terms.	MOUA SG	MC	

	(ii) Allow higher floor Area Ratio for the construction of hotels.		
	(iii) Adopt liberalized floor space index of 2.5/3.0 and		
	(iv) Rationatise stamp duty and rescind capital gains tax in the case of hotel projects.		
	(v) Make land conversions easy and charges reasonable.		
27.	Implement the site management plans parepared World Heritage Centres and major national monuments with the participation of private sector.	ASI MOT	ITDC STDC
28.	Set up way site amenities at every 100 kms. On high way connecting important tourist places.	MOST,SG MOT MOP	BP HP IO
29.	All new petrol pumps must have one public amenities.	P & NG SG	

30.	Establish one modern Souvenir shop at all major tourist attraction places. Items kept could be especially designed with the help of National Insitute of Design and other similar institutions.	MOC ASI MOT	
31.	Undertake integrated development of heritage sites with private sector funding as in the case of Shanwar Wada project of Pune.	ASI MOT SG	
32.	Prepare tourism development plans for the following National Parkes/ Wild life Sancturaries with conservations as primary goal and implement such plans with the assistance of private sector : (i) Bandhavgarh (ii) Bandipur (iii) Bharatpur (iv) Corbett (v) Gir (vi) Kanha (vii) Kaziranga (viii) Little Rann of Kutch	MOEF MOT SG	STDC

	(ix) Mudumali (x) Nagarhole (xi) Periyar (xii) Ranthambore (xiii) Sariska (xiv) Simlipal			
33.	Develop a couple of streets or town squares at frequently visited tourist cities like Agra, Ahmedabad, Jaipur, Lucknow, Varanasi, etc. to preserve and project the distinctive architecture and other features, sanitize the areas, develop hygienic food shops, souvenir stalls, etc. to provide visitors with living attractions of street life.	MOT SG		MC
34.	Develop heritage tourism in the States of Gujrat, Karnataka, kerala, Madhya Pradesh and Tamil Nadu on the lines of Rajashtan by providing financial and fiscal incentives.	MOT SG		TAAI IATD
35.	India Convention Promotion Bureau (ICPB) be activated to build networking	MOT SG	ICPM STDC	H,TA,TO, OPF

	relationship between the partners involved in convention tourism like the hotels, private convention promoters, State Governments, etc.			
36.	Establish convention centres on a regional basis with the assistance of Central Government.	MOT SG	ICPM STDC	H,TA,TO OPF
37.	Take-up the implementation of 5 special Tourism Area project (Bekal), Diu, Mamallapuram, Puri, Sindhudurg) by the Union Ministry of Tourism and expedite development.	MOT	MOT STDC	
38.	Introduce a system for identification, approval and certification of 'Adventure Tourism Products' to assist the potential customers with quality products.	MOT SG	NIWA IISM	IATO TAAI
39.	Set-up an Advanced Institute of Hotel Management and a Culinary Institute.	MOT		H,TA,TO TTO
40.	Set up at least one Food Craft Institute in each State.	MOT SG	NCHMCT AICTE	

41.	Modernise the existing training Institutions in Hotel Management on Catering Technology to a Achieve quality improvement in training.	MOT SG	NCHMCT
42.	Set a target of 5 million foreign tourist arrivals and Rs. 30,000 crores foreign exchange earning within the next five years.	MOT PC	

Abbreviation		Expansion
MOEF	=	Ministry of Environment and Forest
MOH	=	Ministry of Home Affairs
MOT	=	Ministry of Tourism
MOCA	=	Ministry of Civil Aviation
RBI	=	Reserve Bank of India
SG	=	State Governments
Rlys	=	Railways
ASI	=	Archaeological Survey of India
MOST	=	Ministry of Surface Transport
H	=	Hotels
TA	=	Travels Operators
TTO	=	Tourist Transport Operators
AAI	=	Airport Authority of India
ITDC	=	India Tourism Development Corporation
STDC	=	State Tourism Development Corporation

AL	=	Airlines
OPF	=	Other Private Firms
PC	=	Planning Commission
AISA	=	Air India Sales Agents
MOEA	=	Ministry of External Affairs
SCI	=	Shipping Corporation of India
IWAI	=	Inland Water Authority of India
MOH	=	Ministry of Home
MOUA	=	Ministry of Urban Affairs
MC	=	Municipal Corporation
TSA	=	Time Share Association
NIWS	=	National Institute of Water Sports
IISM	=	Indian Institute of Skiing and Mountaineering
TFCI	=	Tourism Finance Corporation of India
AA	=	Alliance Air
PA	=	Private Airlines
MOIB	=	Ministry of Information and Broad Casting
MOF	=	Ministry of Finance
MOP	=	Ministry of Petroleum
AI	=	Air India
IA	=	Indian Airlines
ICPA	=	Indian Convention Promotion Bureau
WTTC	=	World Travel and Tourism Council
IB	=	Intelligence Bureau
DGCA	=	Directorate General of Civil Aviation
WLI	=	Wild Life Institute
NCHMCT	=	National Council of Hotel

		Management and Catering Technology.
AICTE	=	All India Council of Technogy of Technical Education
INTACM	=	Indian National Trust for Art and Culture Heritage
IITTM	=	Indian Institute of Tourism and Travel Management
ASSCHOM	=	Associate Chamber of Commerce & Industry
FICCI	=	Federation of Indian Chambers of Commerce and Industry.
BP	=	Bharat Petroleum
IO	=	Indian Oil
HP	=	Hindustan Petroleum